Given

by the

Lincoln Christian College

Alumni Association

As Part

of a

$100,000 Gift,

1968-1971

# NOTABLE
# SERMONS FROM
# PROTESTANT
# PULPITS

# NOTABLE SERMONS FROM PROTESTANT PULPITS

Charles L. Wallis, Editor

$\oint$

**ABINGDON PRESS**

NEW YORK • NASHVILLE

NOTABLE SERMONS FROM PROTESTANT PULPITS

*Copyright © MCMLVIII by Abingdon Press*

*Library of Congress Catalog Card Number: 58-9526*

*Printed in the United States of America*

# PREFACE

MANY YEARS AGO SEVERAL COMPETENT AND DISCERNING NATIONAL and church leaders called for a de-emphasis on preaching, or even for what was described as a moratorium in preaching. During the subsequent years no such voice has been raised. Today the Protestant pulpit represents an earnestness, integrity, persuasiveness, quality, and respect which has in recent times seldom been equaled. During these years of crisis and decision, the pulpit has, by and large, offered a sure and steady beacon to an unstable and confused generation, a fearless prophetic witness, a socially concerned emphasis, a devotional testimony, and a genuine hopefulness centered in the life, message, and salvation of Jesus Christ. Today more ministers expound the Word of Life from more pulpits and more laymen find inspiration and guidance in church worship than ever before. The radius of the sermon has ever widened to embrace the moral and social dilemmas of all humanity, and ever deepened to detect the positive will of God. The thin and popular lectures, with their forays into the marginal concerns of evangelic Christianity, have been replaced by the proclamation of the gospel in a manner consistent with the homiletic heritage of the centuries. None of us who proclaim the Word is content or satisfied that the witness of the pulpit equals the need of our times, yet recognition is warranted for the ways by which the burden of the Lord is being borne by those whom God has called to be his interpreters.

The sermons in this collection variously portray the minister as shepherd, teacher, counselor, prophet, and expositor. The individual writers mirror a major preaching emphasis of their week-by-week ministry. These sermons, contributed by invitation, are representative of the articulation of God's Word in the Protestant pulpit.

CHARLES L. WALLIS

5

# CONTENTS

# I

## Christian Growth and Nurture

# PRISONERS OF OURSELVES

*Ralph W. Sockman*

Bring me out of prison, that I may give thanks to thy name!—Ps. 142:7 (R.S.V.)

RECENTLY I WAS RIDING IN A RAILROAD COACH FROM ROCHESTER TO Utica. Two young lads sat a few seats in front of me. Viewed from the rear, they seemed to be looking at the scenery and conversing like the other passengers. Presently it came time for them to leave the train. Then I noticed that they were handcuffed to each other. It is hard to describe the expression of their faces as they walked down the aisle. There was a look of humiliation, touched with bitterness. I tried to think how I should feel if I were led through a staring crowd shackled like a wild animal that could not be trusted with its freedom. Bitter is the shame of being a prisoner of the law.

Another kind of prisoner has been made familiar to us by recent wars. Brave men have been captured by enemy troops and held as prisoners of war. Captive peoples have been confined in prison camps. They have suffered privation, even torture, but they have been under no shadow of shame.

And there is still another class of prisoners. They are not shackled or subjected to public disgrace like prisoners of the law. They are not starved or brainwashed like prisoners of war. They may walk the streets or sit in their homes without any external restraint. Yet they are imprisoned by bars of their own making.

Ps. 142 is headed with this inscription: "A prayer of David when he was in a cave." If, as some think, this psalm voices the mood of David when he was in the cave of Adullam where he was rallying

11

his followers around him, then it is not written from a physical prison. Yet this psalm contains the petition: "Bring me out of prison, that I may give thanks to thy name!" David's spirit was in prison although his body was unfettered. So is it with many a person.

## I

For one thing, some of us may be prisoners of our bodies. Our minds dwell in bodies, and whenever the body gets the upper hand our spirits are imprisoned.

Watch the lithe young girl on the tennis court. How carefree of her body she seems to be. It is just a wonderful instrument to be used in pursuing the sport. Then think of that person fifty years later, and consider how much the concern of her body may have come to dominate her thought and consume her time. The care of the body's health, the coddling of its comforts, the beautifying of its appearance—all this becomes almost a major concern of some people. When this happens it is evident that the body has gotten the better of the spirit. The body, which was meant to be the servant of the spirit, has become its master.

The apostle Paul, sensing this danger, said, "I keep under my body" (I Cor. 9:27). And a little girl, hearing a sermon on that text, reported at home that the minister said, "I keep my soul on top."

Both Paul and the little girl had caught the spirit of Christ, the Great Physician. Jesus has merited the title of the Great Physician not primarily because of the specific illnesses which he cured, but because he put the body in its proper place in the wholeness of life. He did heal men's bodies, but he told them that if they would seek first the kingdom of God, their bodily needs would fall into their proper and secondary place. He would have men keep the right proportion between what they live *on* and what they live *for*. He knew that when persons are fired with a comsuming purpose they become almost indifferent to food and raiment—yes, even to pain. A young couple deeply in love can dwell happily in a modest cottage, whereas when love cools down they are restless in the richest environment.

12

Much as we deplore war and its diabolical devastation, we cannot deny that during war people give less time to coddling their bodies and worrying about their peace of mind. We can see the point and the rebuke in the ex-soldier's remark: "During the war we died *for* things; now we die *of* things." Big purposes free us from petty fretfulness and little ailments.

God can also keep us from being imprisoned by our bodily possessions. We like to surround ourselves with our belongings. It is natural and right to desire nice things around us. Our personalities are in part revealed by the furnishings of our homes. These surroundings show our taste, develop our artistic interests, enlarge our lives. But a house is made to be lived *in* and not to be lived *for*. Some women are better housekeepers than homemakers. Our material possessions are meant to be the scaffolding by which we build more stately mansions for our souls. But they can become our prisons.

We might well heed the words of Hermann Hagedorn:

> Lift up the curtain; for an hour lift up,
> The veil that holds you prisoners in this world
> Of coins and wires and motor-horns, this world
> Of figures and of men who trust in facts
> This pitiable, hypocritic world
> Where men with blinkered eyes and hobbled feet
> Grope down a narrow gorge and call it life.[1]

## II

Our bodies, furthermore, can imprison us by their passions. We know what strong fetters are forged by sinful habit. All about us are the slaves of drink and lust and greed. But around us also are those who can testify with the apostle Paul, "Where sin abounded, grace did much more abound" (Rom. 5:20). They have found how God can so fill men with hope and higher hungers that they are delivered from the bondage of degrading appetite.

We commonly speak of higher education as "liberal education."

[1] Used by permission.

It should liberate us from our limitations. And in this liberating process we should begin with our own bodies and prepare to keep ourselves free from bondage to our pains, our possessions, our passions. A liberal attitude should also keep us from being imprisoned by our *minds*. Milton said:

> The mind is its own place, and in it self
> Can make a Heav'n of Hell, a Hell of Heav'n.[2]

At three-thirty on a recent Sunday morning my telephone rang. A man called asking me to pray for him that he might be able to go to sleep. I did not relish being awakened in the middle of the night to help someone else get to sleep! It is a practice I do not encourage. At first I fear I showed my irritation, but as I listened to the man's pleading I realized that he was in a mental hell.

Such a case, of course, is extreme. But each Sunday in some of our churches we repeat the prayer of general confession which contains these words: "We have erred and strayed from thy ways like lost sheep." We human beings so easily become like sheep. We become herd-minded. We browse along with our heads down, nibbling at the little ideas next to us. When our minds thus go along with the herd, we drift into the dead ends of narrow prejudice and the dangers of perverted desire.

We need divine help to lift us out of our herd-mindedness. Even college graduates can become blind followers of empty slogans unless they stop, look, and listen at the crossings where the timely meets the timeless. In this age of specialization we can be misled by small clever minds that know their own lines, but do not see how the specialties fit into the patterns of larger living. One reason for infusing education with religion is to help men see life steadily and see it whole.

When we get the larger, liberating outlook we distinguish between the transient and the lasting. Charles Ranson recalls an interesting bit of history. In 1903, Lord Curzon was Viceroy of India. He organized an immense durbar in Delhi to celebrate the

[2] From *Paradise Lost*, Bk. I, ll. 254-55.

accession of Edward VII to the British imperial throne. A religious service was planned. Lord Curzon asked to see the program in advance. He found that one of the hymns was "Onward, Christian Soldiers." He exercised his viceregal veto and took out that hymn. Why? Not because most of the native soldiers participating were Moslems and Hindus, but because the hymn contained the lines:

> Crowns and thrones may perish,
> Kingdoms rise and wane.

Lord Curzon apparently could not envisage a state of affairs in which the British Crown which he represented could possibly wane in India. Yet within fifty years the Indian Empire gave way to a free republic within the commonwealth.

Also, the divine touch liberates the mind to see over barriers which at the moment may seem insurmountable. Listen to these words:

> Between them there is nothing in common either in object, interest or feeling—nothing that apparently tends to their connection unless it be the waters that flow between them. And even these waters, instead of in fact uniting them, form a barrier between them which, however frequently passed, still form and must forever continue to form an insurmountable obstacle to their union.

Does not that quotation sound like a devastating argument against the possibility of uniting the nations? But those words were not written lately to prove the unworkability of the United Nations. According to Halford E. Luccock of Yale, those words were written in 1833 to prove the impossibility of ever joining the village of Brooklyn to the city of New York! Yet the barrier of the East River did not prove forever insurmountable. Fifty years later the Brooklyn Bridge was built and today the subway joins the Brooklynites and the Manhattanites.

In my boyhood, when my father wished to describe anything beyond the bounds of possibility he would say, "We can no more do that than fly to Egypt." Yet we now fly to Egypt in less than twenty-four hours. And even in more recent times, the last word in describing the impossible was to speak of flying to the moon. Yet Harold Wessman, dean of the Engineering College at the University of Washington, wrote recently:

With rocket engines which do not need air for fuel, with nuclear energy as a source of power, with metals of high strength, with refractory linings of high heat-resistance, with radar as the navigation and communications aid, travel to the moon, 238,000 miles away, does not seem to be a fantastic dream.

It is not romantic dreaming to predict that the youth of today may see the day when flights to the moon are possible. It is not scientific to set fixed limits to the advances of our physical sciences. But the human race will set a limit to its own survival unless it speeds up the development of its spiritual power to match its horse power. With the hydrogen bomb to give him power and the jet plane to give him proximity to his neighbor, man now for the first time in history could commit race suicide. But there are signs that we are waking up to the peril of racial destruction in time to ward it off. The growing demand for some measures of disarmament, the increasing programs of economic assistance, the rising tide of religious interest throughout Christendom and beyond—all these make global war less likely today than at any time since 1945.

Familiar is George Frederick Watts's painting, "Hope." A dejected female figure sits limply atop the globe of the world. Her back is bent as though every muscle had surrendered to circumstance. Her head is bowed as though the eye would see no more of sorrow. She is clutching a lyre whose strings are broken. As one looks at this bent figure cowering over the broken instrument in semidarkness, he wonders with Gilbert Keith Chesterton why the picture is not called "Despair" instead of "Hope." And then he sees that one string is not broken. And with Chesterton, "he knows that there is something in man which is always apparently on the eve of disappearing, but never disappears. . . . He knows a great moral fact . . . that faith is always a perpetually defeated thing which survives all its conquerors."

## III

Thirdly, if we are truly liberal, our hearts as well as our bodies and minds must be liberated.

When doors are slammed against us, we are prone to draw into ourselves and lock our hearts against others. When others give us the cold shoulder, we turn to them a cold back. When we know that another dislikes us or suspects us, we are likely to do things which tend to arouse more dislike or suspicion. Thus distrust begets distrust. Thus hearts freeze up into prisons of the soul.

Some time ago I heard of a lad who was failing in his school work. He rebelled against going. He would not study. He was considered a problem child. An experienced boys' worker who was called into the situation discovered that the lad's spirit had somehow been hurt and he had developed an inferiority complex. His school was changed and confidence was shown toward him. His inventive interests were stimulated, and now his imprisoned energies are free and active.

Observe the same hardening of hearts between nations and races. Iron curtains tend to make steel hearts. Two nations hide behind their barriers and each imagines dire things being planned and done by the other. And unless some doors of understanding can be opened, distrust develops into cold war and may even burst into hot fighting.

In one of his last speeches before the House of Commons, before he gave up his premiership, Sir Winston Churchill spoke of the way in which the entire foundation of human affairs has been revolutionized by the hideous power which science has placed in the hands of men. And he asked, "Which way shall we turn?" He said: "I find it poignant to look at youth in all its activities and ardor and most of all to watch little children playing their merry games, and wonder what would lie before them if God wearied of mankind."

Our ground of hope is that God does not weary of mankind. And our best way of breaking out of our imprisoning hearts is to draw on the unwearying love of God. We need ever to be reminded of God's measureless mercies toward us.

> There's a wideness in God's mercy,
> Like the wideness of the sea;
> There's a kindness in His justice,
> Which is more than liberty.[3]

And when Christ bade us love our enemies, he gave us this incentive: "That you may be sons of your Father who is in heaven; for he makes his sun rise on the evil and on the good, and sends rain on the just and on the unjust" (Matt. 5:45 R.S.V.).

We need this grace of God to keep our hearts free from resentment against those who wrong us. A white reporter once sought an interview with Roland Hayes, the great Negro singer. He found him in a dingy room where he was eating his meal because the hotel denied him a better place of dining. The reporter exploded in anger, but Hayes said:

> My earliest teacher in voice, himself a Negro, told me that as an artist, a black artist, I would suffer terribly if I allowed the barbs to penetrate my soul; but if my heart was right, and my spirit divinely disciplined, then nobody in all the world would be able to hurt me. I know now that this is true. I try every moment of every day to live in such awareness of the divine that no bitterness can creep into my heart. Thus I have learned how to be happy, and I have discovered that nobody in all the world can hurt me except myself.

When a person can attain such an attitude, he has escaped from the imprisoning bitterness of mind and heart. In the words of Henry van Dyke:

> Self is the only prison that can ever bind the soul;
> Love is the only angel who can bid the gates unroll;
> And when he comes to call thee, arise and follow fast;
> His way may lie through darkness, but it leads to light at last.[4]

---

[3] Frederick W. Faber.
[4] "The Prison and the Angel," from *The Poems of Henry van Dyke*, copyright 1920 by Charles Scribner's Sons.

# 2

# THE PLACE OF LOCAL LOYALTIES

*Theodore Parker Ferris*

> If I forget thee, O Jerusalem, let my right hand
> forget her cunning.—Ps. 137:5

WHEN YOU THINK OF THE CIRCUMSTANCES UNDER WHICH THAT LINE was written, you may ask: Wouldn't it have been better if he *had* forgotten Jerusalem? He was a Jew living in forced exile in Babylonia. Jerusalem, largely destroyed, was hundreds of miles behind him. The chances of his ever seeing it, let alone living in it again, were very slight. Wouldn't it have been better if he and his fellow Jews had left the local loyalty completely behind them and marched out into the greater loyalties of the new and larger world that spread before them?

This text, strangely enough, came to my mind on a Sunday morning when I was in Paris. I had planned, not too deliberately but more or less definitely, to go that Sunday morning to High Mass in Notre Dame. I love the building and I have learned through experience that the only time to see the great churches of Europe is on Sundays, when they are no longer museums but have become churches once again, and the tourists are at least partially restrained. I had never been in Notre Dame for a service on Sunday, and I wanted very much to go. I got up with every intention of going. I knew that I could not go to that service and also to the service of my own church in the American Cathedral because they were at approximately the same time.

When it came time for me to start out for the service, I began to waver. I felt somehow strongly drawn to my own church, to the service that I would know and find familiar in the English

19

language and according to the Book of Common Prayer, and to people whom I would almost surely know and like to see. I ended up of course by going to my own American church. As I walked toward it, my mind was not completely at rest and I kept saying to myself something like this: You are just like all the other Americans you criticize; you are provincial, you are parochial. Here you are away from home; why not forget for the time being your local loyalties, and immerse yourself in greater world-wide interests, both in religion and in national life? Forget that you are an American, that you are an Episcopalian and a Protestant—at least for the time being—and launch out into deeper, wider waters. Then this text came to my mind: "If I forget thee, O Jerusalem, let my right hand forget her cunning." The words set my mind at rest, and I went to the service and never had a more satisfying, fulfilling hour of public worship anywhere.

I

This little incident, unimportant as it is, raised in my mind the whole subject—and it is a big subject; big because like all great subjects it has two sides, and those sides are often contradictory and paradoxical—the subject of the place of local loyalties in a man's life. Have they any place at all, and if they do, what is it?

I began to think about the subject by thinking about people, because this is the way we normally approach things, not theoretically, abstractly, but dramatically in terms of personality. I thought of people like Charles William Eliot. He was born in Boston and died in Cambridge, not very far away. He lived within a few miles of the State House of Massachusetts for ninety-two years. He was educated at Harvard, he taught at Harvard, and was the president of Harvard University for forty years. It would be hard to think of anyone so completely immersed in local loyalties, so completely committed to a particular task in a particular spot. And yet someone like John Jay Chapman, who remembered him, could write about him after he died that he was known to every man in America and many in Europe. Chapman goes on to say in his essay on Eliot that before Eliot's time no one used to ask who the president of Harvard was. After his time, the president of Harvard was a national figure, and the president of every other university in the land was a figure to be reckoned with. Here was a man with nationwide influence, who was committed to intensely local loyalties.

Then I thought of a person like William Temple, who was born in England and died in England. His father was archbishop of Canterbury; he was archbishop of Canterbury, a student at Oxford, and a don at Oxford. You might almost say that he was the incarnation of Anglicanism. You cannot imagine anybody who could incorporate more of what the Church of England is than William Temple. And yet I think that if you ask anybody who knows much about the birth and coming into being of the World Council of Churches, he would say that the man who inspired it perhaps more than any other was this intensely English clergyman, William Temple—a person with local loyalties, bound up in them, and yet with world-wide influence and world-wide interests.

Another person I thought of was Shakespeare. As far as we know, he never left the shores of England in his whole life. You might say that his mature life was bounded by the city limits of London and the walls of the Globe Theater. Yet he has revealed the heights and depths of human nature, not only to Englishmen, but to people all over the globe; not only to the seventeenth century, but also to the twentieth century man. It is the intensity of his local commitment that has produced the extensiveness of his world-wide influence.

I thought of many others, and you can think of others equally well known. Wendell Willkie, so intensely American, and yet leading us to think about world government; Robert Frost, so intensely a New Englander, and yet speaking not only to all America but to the whole English-speaking world. However, that is enough for the people.

Then I began to draw some conclusions, and the first obvious conclusion is that there *is* a place for local loyalties in a man's life. Indeed, a man is a little like a tree. A tree has to be planted before it can spread its branches. A man has to be rooted in something before he can reach for the moon. We should never forget that. In fact, you never find a world-wide interest that is not grounded in some local loyalty. You never find a man who loves the world in general who does not love some little spot of the world in particular. You never find, I think, a man or a woman who loves family life in general who is not committed to some one family for which he would gladly die. You never find a man who is interested in world politics who is not interested in the political life and social life of his own town. You might almost say that a man becomes universal to the degree to which he is willing to be provincial.

Remember, therefore, Jerusalem. Remember the local loyalties of your life that are like cradles in which and out of which you grow. We who can be so mobile and move so fast and so easily that we can be in many places at almost the same time need this word from the Old Testament: Remember Jerusalem, remember your home. Don't have so many homes that you are never in any one of them long enough to make it a home. Remember your town, remember your church. Hold and cultivate the local loyalties of your life. Without them your branches are not likely to spread far.

## II

That is one side of the subject. There are two sides. The side that we have already considered is the comfortable side. The other side is the uncomfortable side. I began to think about this side by thinking about people—in this case, about one person in particular, Robert E. Lee. He is one of the monumental Americans, one of my heroes, one whom many have come to appreciate as his character and life have been more and more unfolded by people like Douglas Freeman.

In the middle of the nineteenth century he was a colonel in the United States Army, stationed in Texas, trying to keep in line the Mexicans across the border. Trouble was brewing over the slavery issue. Secession was in the air. Lee, even though he was a Southerner, was against the principle of secession and in favor of the Constitution and loyalty to it. He wrote to one of his friends:

The framers of our Constitution never exhausted so much labor, wisdom and forbearance in its formation, and surrounded it with so many guards and securities, if it was intended to be broken by every member of the Confederacy at will.

He was against the principle of slavery. He wrote to another friend, "If I owned four million slaves, I would cheerfully sacrifice them for the preservation of the Union." The thing that he dreaded happened. Texas voted for secession—one hundred and sixty-six to seven—and he was sent home to Virginia. As he went, he feared that Virginia might do the same thing. In a letter to a friend he confessed that (remember now what I have said about his principles) : "he had ever been taught that his first allegiance was due his mother state, and that under no circumstances could he ever bear his sword against Virginia's sons."

You know what happened in that tragic course of events, and you know what he decided to do. At the end of a review of the biography, *Gray Fox*, there is this line: "He belonged to the nation—but to Virginia first." I wish it could have been written the other way. I wish it could have been written: "He belonged to Virginia—but to the nation first." I think the great man was wrong. I am not in a position to make any judgment upon him and, if I had been in his place, I very well might have done the same thing; but in the light of history and against the background of all we understand to be the imperative demands made upon us to reach up from the local loyalties to the greater ones, I say humbly that I think he was wrong.

Local loyalties that do not lead upward and outward to greater ones, more universal ones, more unearthly ones, in the long run are fatal. They suffocate the person who holds them and ultimately strangle him. This may seem a long way from us but I am not sure that it is. I do not know how to suggest this with sufficient pointedness to show it as a principle to be applied not only in judgment of other people, but to yourself. The man who applies it to other

23

people *before* he has applied it to himself has missed it completely.

Perhaps I might put it this way: There are times when the local loyalties are forgotten in order that, or because, other things may be remembered. For instance, there are times, and this is one of them, when the members of political parties must forget the party and remember the principles that they stand for when they are tempted to think of compromising their principles in order to win votes. This is not easy to do. This is a time when we remember the things that are bigger than either party. There are times, and this is one of them, when Americans may have to forget America, so to speak, and remember the world and its needs, its interdependence; remember that other people need oil just as much as we do, and that we make mistakes just as other countries have made them. There are times when Episcopalians may have to forget that they are Episcopalians and remember the Church of Christ at large in the world, with all its manifold branches, all different, but nevertheless all parts of one body, acknowledging one Lord, the God and Father of us all. There are times when you may have to forget your own little nest, your cubbyhole in life, where life is comfortable, and to which you are rightly and naturally loyal, in order to remember some word or some principle that has come to you from God.

## III

This is hard, and do not let anyone make you think it is otherwise. It is easy to talk about other people doing it, but it is terribly hard when you try to do it yourself. The only help that I know of comes from Jesus. He was born, he lived and died in a little land no larger than the state of Vermont. He never went outside it. When he sent out his young apprentices to preach his gospel, he told them to preach to the lost sheep of the house of Israel. He never went out of it, yet he went down so deep into it that his local loyalties were inevitably led upward and outward into greater and more universal loyalties, his loyalty to the kingdom of God.

When he saw it for the first time with his parents, I am sure that he loved Jerusalem. I am sure he loved it as a young man when he came up to it from his country hill-town and saw the golden spires on the white marble walls of the temple. I am sure he loved it when he went up to it the last time and wept over it, and said, "O Jerusalem, Jerusalem, you have had so many chances, so many chances, and you have refused them all, and now your house is left unto you desolate." And yet, the time came when he could not remain loyal to Jerusalem as it then existed and be loyal also to the higher things that belonged to the kingdom of God. When that time came, he had to forget Jerusalem because he remembered God.

# 3

# CHOSEN FOR HOLINESS

*John L. Casteel*

> He hath chosen us in him before the foundation
> of the world, that we should be holy and without
> blame before him.—Eph. 1:4

ON THIS GRAND DIMENSION GOD PROPOSES TO CUT THE PATTERN OF
our life. Beyond all we are able to hope or to think, he intends for
us a destiny and a character which alone can fit us to enter into
his own life, and to have part in his own illimitable purposes.
Breathless as often we are today before the changes wrought in the
circumstances of our living by the miracles of science, we are ex-
horted still to wait for the marvels which are soon to come. Yet
these wonders, which now are transforming the outward fashion
of our living, are inconsequential beside the transformation God
purposes in our own selves. We ought to fix our expectant eyes
upon this great promise, with its declaration of his intention for
all who acknowledge him and accept his love: "He hath chosen
us . . . before the foundation of the world, that we should be holy
and without blame before him."

## I

Toward the idea of holiness we have contradictory feelings.
We do not easily understand what the word means. The thought
is too much for us. Like a counterfeit coin it often connotes of
people who, as we say, assume a "holier-than-thou" attitude. Their
pose suggests a self-conscious piousness that prides itself on its own
virtue while it fails in charity toward the shortcomings of others.
But holiness as a positive good, as an attribute of God himself,

bestowed upon those whom he chooses, lies beyond our common thought. We do not know what to make of it.

Again, the more we do come to understand true holiness, the more difficult for us to believe that it can be possible. No unsuspecting winner of the jackpot, in our day of grand surprises, knows anything like the amazement which floods in upon the person who awakens one day to this great gift which God has prepared for him: to be holy and without blame before him. Too good to be true, the thought of it taxes the power of our poor minds to claim it for our own.

Still more—and with shame we sometimes come to confess it—holiness speaks of a quality of life we do not always wish to have, even as God's gift. Like inept and irresponsible people who move from a city slum to the clean countryside, and turn even that pleasant scene into a clutter-heap, we take the brightest of our possibilities and spoil them to suit our old ways, our old nature. The slum is inside of us. To be holy would strip us of our self-chosen indulgences, our low arrangement of the manner of our life. And we are not sure we are willing to give these up. Blameless we are anxious to appear in our own eyes, and we spend no amount of time, of talk, of inward energies to maintain ourselves as blameless in the sight of others. But to be without blame and holy in God's eyes would require us at the very outset to surrender our stubborn effort to appear so to ourselves. We cannot easily believe in holiness because we do not wish to believe in it. It is not only too good, but too demanding, too painful to our old selves, to be true.

Yet we never can quite give up the hope that we may be meant for such a destiny and purity of life. We yearn to be holy. We long to think that we may someday become quite different—finer, purer, truer, than we now are. Browning has his Rabbi Ben Ezra say:

> What I aspired to be,
> And was not, comforts me.

That will do for the trivial ambitions and the juvenile aspirations of our past. But what we deeply aspire to be, and are not—for this

27

most of us need to be comforted. We survive almost every griev-
ance life throws upon us but this: that we fail to be right in the
sight of God. Like the poor woman in Léon Bloy's novel, we come
down to the wearied end of our years saying: "There is but one
sadness, and that is for us not to be saints!" [1]

Holy and without blame we are not; holy and without blame
God may intend us to be, although we cannot or will not believe
it; but holy and without blame before him we yearn to be with
unquenchable longing—and we are never at peace until in some
measure this shall become true for us, of us, in us.

## II

What is this holiness for which God has chosen us? No definition seems able to express our meaning. We apprehend that holiness has to do with God himself and cannot be thought of apart
from him. To be holy is to be like God, sharing to the limit of
our poor human powers in his purity, righteousness, love, and
eternal life.

Holiness comes into our lives because we have been with God.
In our common phrase, something of him "rubs off" onto us just
as something of the life and quality of another person colors us
through our association with him. Our children tramp home from
an afternoon of play on the neighborhood lot, and we know at
once who their playmates have been. Our young people come
home from college, and without asking, we perceive something
of the kind of young people who have been their roommates and
classmates. From day to day by necessity, indifference, or choice,
we work, visit, and company with others; and carry about with us
the aura of their lives. The strange and powerful element in
every person is his capacity both to give off and to tolerate and
receive a quality of essential being. Most completely does this
truth work out when we come into touch with God, who is
Infinite Person. We are made holy by having been with him.

But we company with him and partake of his holiness not because of our own purposes and efforts, but, as our text declares,

[1] *Le Femme Pauvre*, quoted in *Pilgrim of the Absolute*, ed. Raissa Maritain
(New York: Pantheon Books, 1947), p. 299.

because he has chosen us. Throughout the first chapter of the epistle in which the text appears the initiative on God's part is asserted over and over. The verbs pile up. It is God who has blessed, chosen, predestined, counseled, made, abounded toward, made known, and purposed us—he who has appointed us to be the objects and recipients of his grand design. There is not a word here to encourage us in thinking that the outcome will be brought about through our desire or ambition.

One of the self-authenticating truths which we come at last to acknowledge is this strange fact: that we know that for the evil in our lives we ourselves are responsible, but for the good God alone deserves the praise. Never is this truth more convincing to us than when we confront the man who claims to have acquired goodness by his own efforts. We cannot avoid the judgment that this claim to self-achieved goodness seems somehow to be the last triumph of evil in him! Whatever true goodness he may have, has come to him only by the grace of God.

Nor is this initiative on God's part a casual gesture of good will. And his action toward us is charged with his passionate and infinite love. The vision of God given us in Jesus Christ always has this double dimension, that in Christ we see not only the *kind* of action God undertakes in order to bring us to himself, but we feel also the *intensity* of the love which prompts and informs all God does. "For he lingered not," wrote Augustine, "but ran calling aloud by words, deeds, death, life, descent, ascension; crying aloud to us to return to him!" So the love of God in Christ had overtaken and captured and made ready in holiness his own dark and troubled soul.

The experience of our common days proves that love to us. In the midst of our ordinary affairs God breaks in upon us and we learn, sooner or later, that the most inexorable fact of our life is simply that he is never going to leave us alone. Like the wedding guests, suddenly we find ourselves conscript in his presence and unfit to stand there, but he clothes us and bids us sit at the feast. Penitent and wretched in some night we dare creep only to the outmost courts of his holy abiding place, but he hears us and in mercy sends us home justified, at peace with him

29

and with ourselves. Embarrassed when he walks into the midst of our business we cannot but invite him home to dinner, and before he enters we make our pledge to put right all this calculating and sharp dealing by which we've been striving to get on so comfortably and to make ourselves so secure against the future. With a relentlessness that only love can sustain, day in and day out, he chooses and keeps choosing us, and will not let us go until we are entered upon the way which will bring us at last to stand holy and without blame before him.

### III

If such be God's purpose for us, and if only his action toward us can bring it to pass, nevertheless, we have our part to fulfill, our responsibility for which to answer. Even God does not invade our lives without respect for the integrity of our will and being. The fulfillment of his will for us waits upon our will to choose him above all else. God alone can make us holy and blameless; but we have the responsibility to see that he is free to bring this about.

We are to discharge that responsibility by stretching our faith concerning the reality of this holiness he intends us to receive. If holiness seems strange and unreal to us, is it not because we have thought of it so little or stirred our hunger for it so seldom? Here, as in every sphere of human advancement, we arrest our growth by concluding that no one can go farther than the point at which we have now arrived. Then one day someone *does* "break through the barrier," and after him others of us go on to the fulfillment of what was once regarded as impossible. A violinist of Beethoven's time complained that one of the composer's quartets was too difficult for performance. The great genius shouted back, "Does he really suppose I think of his little fiddle when the spirit speaks to me and I compose something?" But other violinists did manage to play it, and today it belongs in the repertoire of every reputable string quartet.

And in our own small, unexciting, unexceeding lives, we have found ourselves sometimes doing the impossible, because some emergency forced us, or some believing love inspired us, to try and to do what we so long had known never could be done at all.

Imagination, desire, and faith had to be roused for us until we began to think the unreal might indeed become the real!

Can any prediction for us be more fantastic, more defiant of common sense and common experience, than the claim made for us in the text? Yet some have stretched their minds to comprehend that it could be true; and some have stirred up the longing of their hearts to hope passionately that it might be true; and some have made the venture of faith that it shall be true. And they have not been disappointed nor deceived. "Great God!" cried Fénelon, "Can we think that something of the life of Jesus Christ may be known in us!" [2] The answer of all those who have opened themselves to receive the gift of God is: "Yes, he is able to do exceeding abundantly above all we can ask or think!" To be chosen of God for holiness we must first come to believe that holiness is possible. We must set our minds upon it, yearn for it, have faith in what God can bring about in us.

But this stretching of imagination, this stirring of desire and rousing of our wills does not give us leave to indulge in a kind of spiritual daydreaming. If God has indeed chosen us to be holy and without blame before him we are required then to live, as far as in us lies, day by day in the confidence that his purpose can be true and real for us. Ranier Rilke wrote of the great French sculptor, Auguste Rodin, that during his early years of study in Brussels, he could be seen walking down the streets of that city as though greatness awaited him round the corner. Our calling is like that: to go through the affairs and duties, the work and the repose of our life, as though holiness waited for us at the next turn.

From that center of responsibility we will find ourselves making our decisions, ordering the uses of our time, carrying on our trade and labor, loving and nurturing our children, bearing up under the afflictions of life, and always allowing the interior mood and spirit of our selves to be transformed by the spirit of God. We will not suppose at any point that we have attained to the holiness to which we are called. We will not consciously calculate

[2] *Christian Perfection,* tr. Mildred W. Stillman (New York: Harper and Bros., 1947), p. 46.

every work and action as to whether it befits our new condition or advances us cumulatively on our way. To all the well-meant flattery of those who think they know us when they praise us for our virtues, we will reply firmly, as one holy One did before us: "Get behind me! You are flavored with the notions of men, not God!"

But deep within ourselves, if we persevere in patience and fidelity, we will again and again be given some intimation of the work God is bringing to pass in us: the restoration of the clean heart, the re-creation of the right spirit, and the secret growth of his own divine beauty and righteousness within us. And we shall be amazed at his grace, and shall find ourselves possessed of joy which passes understanding.

# 4

# THE GOSPEL AS OFFER A[ND] DEMAND

*Rolland W. Schloerb*

THE CHRISTIAN GOSPEL HAS TWO ASPECTS: ONE IS THE PR[oclama]tion of what has been done for us and the other is the affi[rmation] of what is demanded from us. The Gospel offers somethin[g] but it also demands something from us.

The Bible is full of proclamations of what God has done[.] Isaiah the prophet says: "Sing praises to the Lord, for [he has] done gloriously; let this be known in all the earth." (Isa[.] R.S.V.) In the New Testament we have the reassuring news: [God] so loved the world that he *gave* his only Son, that whoeve[r be]lieves in him should not perish but have eternal life" (John [3:16] R.S.V.). God loved us before we could love him. He did so[me]thing for us before we could do anything for him. This is [the] heart of the good news of our religion.

But God does not do everything. Not everything is done *for* [us.] Something is also demanded *from* us. There is a give-and-take i[n] the Christian life. Paul follows a sound instinct when, after hi[s] shattering experience on the Damascus road, he cries out, "Wha[t] shall I do, Lord?" (Acts 22:10 R.S.V.). He felt that something was demanded of him. The prophet Micah has given us one of the great insights of religion when he says: "He has showed you, O man, what is good; and *what does the Lord require of you* but to do justice, and to love kindness, and to walk humbly with your God?" (Mic. 6:8 R.S.V.). Notice these key words: *What does the Lord require of you?* Religion, as this prophet regarded it, had requirements as well as offers. It not only gives something to us, but it demands something from us.

I

Religious living is impoverished if it emphasizes only one of these aspects to the neglect of the other. In times past there has been a tendency to overemphasize one and to minimize the other. This has been true in the last fifty or one hundred years.

Up to World War I there were many who affirmed that the progress of the world was due to the efforts of man. The part that man played was the important part. Some interpreted evolution as meaning an inevitable upward movement. We were on an escalator that was making life better and better. Man, through education and through science, would accomplish the good life.

Herbert Spencer is often quoted as the high priest of this view of progress:

> Progress is not an accident, not a thing within human control, but a beneficent necessity . . . due to the working of a universal law. So surely must the things we call evil and immorality disappear; so surely must man become perfect.

Man's part in this ladder of progress was emphasized, for the powers of men could and would be the instruments by which progress would be realized.

Then came the reaction. World War I was followed by the wild extremes of the twenties, the devastating depression of the thirties, World War II of the forties, and the cold war of the fifties. The role that man has played is not reassuring. Man has capacities for evil that had never been dreamed of. The violent hatreds and inhumanities and the wholesale slaughter of civilian populations all remind us that man is incapable of building a good world.

The prophets probed beneath our actions to our motives, to those hidden drives that lie below conscious thought. In their individual lives and in their corporate actions men can say with Paul: "I do not understand my own actions. For I do not do what I want, but I do the very thing I hate" (Rom. 7:15 R.S.V.). If we must rely only upon the part we do, then we are bankrupt indeed.

So we have come to a day when there is greater emphasis upon the role of God. We are completely dependent upon the mercy of God. If our religion only proclaims a high standard of ethics, then our religion is a burden heavier than we can bear. Like Paul, we know that no one is made righteous by the law or by relying on his capacity to live up to the requirements of the law. We are dependent on the forgiving mercy of God. We are ultimately saved by what he has done, rather than by what we can do. Little wonder that there has been a return to Protestant theology that is based on the message of the New Testament, "By grace you have been saved through faith" (Eph. 2:8 R.S.V.). God's offer is what is important—the part we do is always tainted by imperfection.

## II

In our time, therefore, we need to remember that there are two sides to the gospel. The gospel is an offer of what God does for us, but it continues also to be a demand upon us. We cannot rest back and say that everything is done by God and nothing can be done by us. The Christian life is both a grateful acceptance by faith of what God has done for us, and it is a dedication of ourselves to what is expected from us.

Paul uses an expression that brings these two thoughts together. He says, "Work out your own salvation with fear and trembling." (Phil. 2:12 R.S.V.) The word "work" in this connection refers to working gold out of mines. We do not put the gold into the hills. That has been done for us and before us. But neither is the gold handed to us in a refined state. We must work it. There is a part for us to do, just as there was a part that was done for us.

An application of this thought may help us to see how the gospel is both offer and demand. The petition of the Lord's Prayer, "Forgive us our debts, as we also have forgiven our debtors," implies one of the greatest offers of our religion, divine forgiveness. God is pictured as one who does not hold our sins against us forever. He is ready to forgive and to release us from the burden of guilt and from the plague of endless self-reproach. The anxiety which stems from a sense of guilt can cripple our activity and warp our outlook upon life. Anything that gives us the peace of forgiveness is a cure for one of the deepest anxieties to which man is heir.

Notice, however, that this petition in the Lord's Prayer also suggests a demand from us. God not only offers to forgive us, but he expects us to forgive one another. In fact, the petition is so stated that the person who is unforgiving cannot expect to enter into the experience of being forgiven. The offer of forgiveness implies the demand that we must be forgiving. It is neither an offer without a demand, nor a demand without an offer. The good news is that he who is forgiving may also experience being forgiven.

The upper room on the eve of the crucifixion was the time when, amid the tense atmosphere of their struggle for status, Jesus washed the disciples' feet. He did the menial service that none of them wanted to perform. Then he said: "You call me Teacher and Lord; and you are right, for so I am. If I then, your Lord and Teacher, have washed your feet, you also ought to wash one another's feet." (John 13:13-14 R.S.V.) In other words, he says that as I have served you, so you are to serve one another.

What an offer is expressed in these actions of Jesus! He did not use and exploit his followers. He did not, first of all, demand that they serve him. He loved them, willingly served them. That is the offer of true greatness. But his offer is not without a demand. The offer and the demand are both recognized when the church celebrates Maundy Thursday during Holy Week. On that night the church is reminded of the commandment (*mandatum*) that Jesus gave to his friends: "A new commandment I give to you, that you love one another even as I have loved you, that you also love one another" (John 13:34 R.S.V.). If we have been loved, we need also to love. Otherwise we become only the pampered children of an indulgent God. The kind of love he gives demands mercy and justice on our part toward each other.

Arthur H. Compton, writing on "The Case for Hope" in *The Saturday Review,* questioned the goals toward which men should aspire. He reminded us of the ancient Greek ideals of the understanding of truth, the appreciation of beauty, and the striving for perfection. He said that these goals are as significant today as they were 2,500 years ago.

Then he adds, "What is new is that in our effort to attain the true, the beautiful, and the good we find that now to a greater degree this can best be done when we endeavor to attain these same objectives for others as well as for ourselves." [1] Our hope of receiving the goods of life lies in our willingness to work that others may receive them too.

This thought is another reminder that with every offer there is a demand. A woman recently commented on a conversation she had with her Roman Catholic neighbor. Her neighbor said: "I sometimes wish I were a Protestant. Your religion seems so easy. There is nothing you must do. In our religion we must go to church and must give to the church. All you have to do is to believe."

If her statement is true, then Protestants are forgetting that the gospel is both offer and demand. The offer calls forth our faith and its grateful acceptance, but it also reminds us that faith without works is dead. Thank God for what has been done for us, and thank God that something is demanded from us! If we are offered forgiveness, it is demanded that we must be forgiving. If we are loved, it is demanded that we also love. The full gospel is best expressed in these simple words: "Freely ye received, freely give" (Matt. 10:8 A.S.V.) .

[1] June 18, 1955, p. 9.

# 5

# THINGS THAT CANNOT BE BORROWED

## *Hampton Adams*

THE POINT OF THE PARABLE OF THE TEN VIRGINS IS THAT THERE are some things that cannot be borrowed. The oil which the five wise virgins held in reserve for a crisis symbolizes this. They did not and could not share their reserves with the foolish virgins.

The twenty-fourth and twenty-fifth chapters of Matthew, constructed as a single discourse, deal with the end of the age and the judgment of Christ. Three parables of Jesus stress the main truths concerning this judgment. The parable of the ten virgins enforces the necessity of a personal, inner preparation. The parable of the talents emphasizes the necessity of a faithful stewardship. The parable of the last judgment unfolds the nature of the love that is required.

The story of the virgins made a vivid picture, for a wedding party was one of the great festivities in Palestinian villages. Men were released from their work, children were let out of their synagogue school, women hurried through their household chores, and all went to the wedding and remained for the celebration. This was not only a privilege, but a duty.

The high point of the wedding came when the bridegroom took the bride from her father's house to their new home. That is where this parable picks up the story. The neighborhood girls are waiting for the bridegroom to bring his bride home. There was a long delay and drowsiness came upon them. They were awakened at midnight by the announcement that the bridegroom was arriving. Five of the girls, seeing that their lamps were almost extinguished, asked the others to share oil with them. This they could not do, so the foolish virgins were forced to seek more oil. While they were gone the brief celebration took place without them.

The refusal of the wise virgins to share their oil may seem harsh, but the story was told by Jesus to make the people see that in a time of crisis there are some things that cannot be borrowed. The oil is symbolic of such things.

We may be surprised to learn of some of the things we cannot borrow.

## I

*We cannot borrow the Bible.*

Of course, you could borrow from your neighbor a copy of the Bible, but actually—if he is a Christian who has lived with his Bible, reading it daily, marking passages in which the word of God seemed to speak directly to him, memorizing much, holding the meaning and promise of much more—you can no more borrow his Bible than the foolish virgins could have borrowed the oil of the wise virgins.

Every person must have his own Bible. Strange things happen when a person suddenly tries to borrow a Bible. There is such a thing as having to borrow a Bible that you own, but have not studied or read. Some of the things that can happen are ludicrous —some are tragic.

When I was an undergraduate in college, in my second or third year, a student who lived in an adjoining room had the mumps and was very ill. He thought he was going to die, and he asked me if I would read the Bible to him. The request made me very nervous because I knew very little about the Bible. I asked what part he wanted me to read, but he did not know. I did not know what to read, but somehow the thirteenth chapter of I Corinthians came to my mind. So I found it and started to read to this young fellow. We went along in our reading with proper piety and solemnity until we came to the verse, "When I became a man, I put away childish things." I tried to restrain a laugh, but when a smile broke on his strained countenance both of us broke into laughter. Perhaps God made use of my ignorance of the Bible to help that boy. Anyway he was soon well again.

But our attempts to borrow the Bible do not always turn out so felicitously. In desperation people have turned to it for the word of Life, but it turned back void because they did not know how to find its treasures.

We must have our own Bible, and we have to know our way through it. There must be places marked in it, even as a well of pure water marks the place for refreshment along a desert trail. We must know our Bible so truly that when we do not have it between covers we still have it. When we were going away for a week's vacation several years ago, I deliberately left my Bible behind so that I could discover how much of the Bible I could recall from memory during my daily devotions. This is an exercise that I recommend.

Has it ever been your privilege to leaf through a Bible that some faithful Christian has studied through the years, lived with and underscored? In preparation for the funeral services of some of these people I have taken their own Bibles and read and used what they underscored. In that way I allowed them to speak their faith to the rest of us. You cannot do that with a borrowed Bible. That can be done only when people have made the Bible their own.

## II

*We cannot borrow a prayer book.*

Of course, we can and should avail ourselves of books of prayer. Since I was in seminary I have kept close at hand the more than four-hundred-year-old Book of Common Prayer, one of the great contributions of the Anglican Church to the Christian world. Also I have *The Priest's Prayer Book* of the Roman Catholic Church, *The Standard Prayer Book* of Judaism, and many others. The greatest prayer book is the Bible with the prayers of the prophets and other leaders of Israel, the prayer Psalms, and the prayers of Jesus. We should read many prayers and acquire the language and the spirit of prayer, and make many of the prayers our own.

Yet it is still true that we cannot borrow a prayer book, wait until some crisis or crushing experience to overtake us, and then frantically call for a prayer book to pray. This is what Martin Luther realized when he supplicated, "Grant that I may not pray alone with the mouth; help me that I may pray from the depths of my heart."

One cannot borrow even the Lord's Prayer, merely repeating the words. Until the Lord's Prayer has become our own, we do not really pray when we reiterate the familiar phrases. Our prayers have to be our own. If we do not believe, we cannot pray the prayer of a believer. If our belief is almost swallowed up in doubt, our prayer must be: "Lord, I believe; help thou mine unbelief." If our heart is filled with bitterness, our prayer can hardly be: "Forgive us our debts, as we forgive our debtors." "Genuine prayer," writes Friedrich Heiler, "is the spontaneous expression of one's own experience or at least the fruit of what one has experienced and gained in struggle." [1] Effectiveness in prayer, therefore, comes from our own growing experience of life with God, communion with God. It can no more be borrowed than the foolish virgins could borrow oil when the crisis arose.

### III

*We cannot borrow a church.*

For weddings and funerals people do borrow the church building, the sanctuary. We offer it to them willingly, but in lending it to them we cannot make it their church. There is something pathetic about people who, having no church, come to borrow one, for all that they can borrow is a material structure. What makes the church the church we cannot lend; it cannot be transmitted in a single transaction.

For a church to be our church, we ourselves must declare it as our "Beth-el," house of God, even as Jacob marked the place where he met God.

For a church to be our church, we must have worshiped there, seen Christ lifted up, felt his presence, seen on his face the light of the glory of God. There in that presence we must have confessed our sins and experienced the grace of forgiveness. From that

[1] From *Prayer*, p. xxiii.

presence we must have gone forth, more than once, with renewed strength and courage and peace.

For it to be our church, we must have worked in it and for it. We must have sacrificed that it might be strong in its witness. For the deepest experience of its being our church we must have made a public profession of our faith in it, received baptism, made our marriage vows, seen our babies dedicated, had our faith in the life everlasting affirmed at a service for a loved one who passed into the nearer presence of God.

Palmer Clarkson once told me of seeing a man, who had long been devoted to his church, standing late one night across the street and looking intently at the church. When he was asked why he was there, he said: "I am just looking at my church. I love every stone in it."

## IV

We cannot borrow a church, the Bible, a prayer book, and *we cannot borrow character.*

One of the important truths that was lifted before the people in the Protestant Reformation is that the merits of the saints cannot by any possible process be transferred to anyone else. Character is something that every person has to achieve for himself.

And certainly character cannot be borrowed in these last hours before we face the final judgment. I know that most people, even Christians, try to put from their minds all thoughts of death. Many people who like to boast of their realism do not have the courage to face the reality that there will one day come a time when it will be too late to build character, too late to do the things they know they ought to have done, too late to explore the Christian mystery of a righteousness that is given to a person because of his faith, too late to exercise the faith that casts out fears, too late to lose oneself in self-forgetting service.

This parable ends with a warning from Jesus: "Watch therefore, for you do not know what day your Lord is coming." And you cannot borrow in that critical hour oil for your lamp.

# II

## The Church and Churchmanship

# 6

# FOR SUCH A TIME AS THIS

## *David A. MacLennan*

> Then Mordecai told them to return answer to Esther. "Think not that in the king's palace you will escape any more than all the other Jews. For if you keep silence at such a time as this, relief and deliverance will rise for the Jews from another quarter, but you and your father's house will perish. And who knows whether you have not come to the kingdom for such a time as this?"—Esth. 4:13-15 (R.S.V.)

> He who has an ear, let him hear what the Spirit says to the churches.—Rev. 2:7 (R.S.V.)

To FIND AN ANALOGY EXISTING BETWEEN THE STORY OF ESTHER and the action of a church in our time would be as unfortunate as it would be untrue. This ancient story of how the secular Jewish festival of Purim originated is brave and thrilling enough to hold children from their play and adults from their television. But it is a blend of intense patriotism and understandable skulduggery. Protestants are patriotic, but we assume that skulduggery even of an ecclesiastical nature is unknown among them.

Nevertheless, to each church member Mordecai's question has a personal application: "Who knows whether you have not come to this province of God's kingdom on earth for such a time as this?"

To this familiar scripture let me join a sentence which recurs, like the tolling of a bell, in the book of Revelation: "He who has an ear, let him hear what the Spirit says to the churches."

# I

What is the Spirit saying to the churches in this year of danger and opportunity? If observers from the front line of the spiritual warfare are right, the message is: You, the visible church of Jesus Christ, have come to the kingdom for such a time as this because *you are the body through which the living Lord must do his work among men.* We churchmen and churchwomen have heard it said so often that the sheer wonder and strangeness of the church's character and mission have been blunted for us. One of our able younger theologians, Daniel Jenkins, has written of *The Strangeness of the Church.* He is quite sure that you cannot understand or evaluate the church as you would another institution in society. "It must be considered in the light of the whole history of those who have called themselves the people of God, from Abraham's time to Christ's, and from Christ's time to our own day." [1] When you do this the "strangeness of the Church" strikes you head on. If we define it in the most general way as "the whole company of those who have publicly confessed their allegiance to the God who has revealed himself in Christ," we can say that it is indeed "the most remarkable institution or group of institutions the world has ever seen." But the New Testament insists that it is more than an institution. Despite the weakness and triviality of many modern churches, it is an organism, a living fellowship; the body of Christ animated by his spirit, directed by his mind, acting as an instrument of his loving and redeeming purpose.

Is it not an astonishing, almost incredible thing that fallible, stubborn, weak, and disconcertingly sinful men and women should be the means whereby the great God who draws near to us in Christ should make his design known and works for its fulfillment? In the middle of the third century a practical and intelligent man of middle age named Cyprian was converted to Christ. He became the first general presbyter of Carthage. He is credited with first declaring that there is no salvation outside the church. At first sight we who stand in the reformed church tradition and faith repudiate such a dogma as intolerant, exclusive, and unchristian.

[1] P. 10.

When used as a big stick to wave above cowering heads, it is to be repudiated. In no sectarian sense can it be true. Yet, is there not a sense in which it is true? The church is integral to the gospel. Membership in the church is the expression in terms of this life of the new relationship which men enjoy with God and each other through what Christ has done for them. So the question which is asked by a leader of British Congregationalism, Daniel Jenkins, is not absurd: "Can there be any salvation outside some form of the Church, when the meaning of salvation is the recovery of that right relation to God and neighbors of which the Church is the concrete expression?" [2] Not before but after the Reformation of the church, Martin Luther asserted:

Anyone who is to find Christ must first find the church. How could anyone know where Christ is and what faith in him is unless he knew where his believers are? . . . Now the church is not wood and stone, but the company of people who believe in Christ. . . . Outside the Christian Church there is no truth, no Christ, no blessedness.[3]

Playing a variation on the same theme, John Calvin wrote in his *Institutes:* "There is no excuse for him who spontaneously abandons the external communion of a church in which the Word of God is preached and the sacraments are administered." [4]

Granted that many who should know better, who do know better, give absent treatment to the worship and fellowship of the church. Granted that many Protestants and, one suspects, a considerable number of our separated brethren also, really have Pontius Pilate as their patron and example. You will recall that the Coptic Church includes Pontius Pilate in their list of saints. They canonized him because of his verdict on his most famous prisoner, "I find no fault in this man." It is indeed a thin foundation for such a high rating—for the man who pronounced that verdict delivered Jesus to be crucified. We have come to the kingdom for such a time to confront members of St. Pontius' church with the blunt fact that finding no fault with the Lord

[2] *The Strangeness of the Church*, p. 155.
[3] From *Luther's Works*.
[4] Bk. IV, Chap. I.

47

of life and history is insufficient. As another has said, it is extremely common to find people who say, "I find no fault in this man, but I haven't been to his church for years and I haven't lifted my little finger to help his cause."

But we believe not in the church of St. Pontius, nor in the church of St. Vitus where everything is incessantly hopping, but not to much point. In the words of the venerable Nicene Creed, we "believe one Holy Catholic and Apostolic Church." As one of our World War II chaplains used to say to curious G.I.'s, we are members, ministers of the holy catholic church, according to the Presbyterian order.

## II

What does the Spirit say to the churches? To our churches the Spirit says that we have come to the kingdom for such a time in order that as members of his spiritual body, *we are to proceed on our threefold commission with unflagging ardor, new strategy, and skills.* What is the threefold task? It is evangelism, worship, and service. These omnibus terms carry many meanings. In this sense they are "loaded," charged by the Spirit of God.

Always the Holy Spirit says to the churches: *preach the Word* and proclaim the gospel through pulpit preaching, through person-to-person witness, through continuous use of what we call "audio-visual aids"—the printed word, the radio, television, drama. Most effective of all is the witness of a life lived by the grace of and in the spirit of our Lord Jesus. One of the most interesting inscriptions to be seen in England is on a certain wall in Chester. It reads:

Near this spot on June 20, 1752, Rev. John Wesley, M. A., preached on the occasion of the first of his many visits to this city. O let me commend my Saviour to you. Erected by the Methodists of Chester, 1952.

Is not that the Word being said by the Spirit to all members of the community of the Holy Spirit, the Church? Is it not true that every day we are either commending our Savior, or failing

to do so? If only we could say it, if only we could translate him
with such penetrating, shining words that the ordinary person
could understand him! Offering Christ to our fellows and offering
our fellows to Christ is our major task. Are we not called upon
to be missionaries? Is not the Spirit saying to the laymen of our
churches: "If you have been called by Christ, and you know you
have been, then you are called to be his representatives, his am-
bassadors, his missionaries." As lawyers say, juries discount a
professional witness but are impressed and sometimes completely
convinced by a non-professional. In Christ's service the "rankest
amateur" who thinks his is only a faltering, inadequate presentation is often more successful than the "pro." To those who ignore
the invitation comes the directive: "Go out . . . and compel them
to come in" (Luke 14:23).

Worship is the primary business of the church. "Not first of all
to do anything," said the late archbishop William Temple when
asked what the church's task is, "but to *be* the Church, the redemptive community offering God the adoring love and worship
of her life." We may assent, but we find it hard really to believe
that the great and infinite God needs our poor stammering prayers
or our little offerings of faded flowers. What can we give him that
he does not possess? We can give him our poor hearts and the
service and love of our lives. As we do the miracle is repeated,
"Heaven comes down our souls to greet." But whether we are
aware of any change or not, it is our bounden duty. Every Lord's
Day is a day of obligation for every Christian. "I appeal to you
therefore, brethren, by the mercies of God, to present your bodies
as a living sacrifice, holy and acceptable to God, which is your
spiritual worship." (Rom. 12:1 R.S.V.) Is there any likelier
place in which to offer this sacrifice than at the holy place where
he himself promised to be present with the two or three or more
who meet there in his name?

The Spirit says to the churches, You have been constituted for
the service of God and man. This service will lead you into
strange places. You will be operating in danger zones where erst-
while friends will join implacable foes to criticize and condemn
your "invasion" of areas allegedly not within your jurisdiction or

49

competence. But whoever was promised a safe shelter in Christ's service? If you have not got a cross—a shouldered burden for Christ and for the sake of others, said old Samuel Rutherford— you have not got Christ. For a cross is the first of his gifts. So Christ's ministers in pulpit and pew are commissioned to keep fathers and brethren sensitive to need wherever it may be found. Whether it be to make us better stewards of our money, or of our time, or of our skills and talents, we must keep ringing the changes on the need of meeting changes! One Great Hour of Sharing, Ecumenical Missions, sponsoring "new" Americans coming to us from overseas lands, striving with dynamic love to rescue our brothers from the degradation of being second-class citizens because of color or race—whatever the call—the Spirit keeps sounding it until we respond with something of the sacrificial support which ought to mark the service of Christians.

### III

To this end, the spirit of God cries to the churches, Go forward with new strategy and in undiscourageable hope. You are not an Ark of Salvation, a refuge from the storms of life. The church does not exist primarily for the edification and comfort of its members. It exists primarily to be an instrument for the extension of God's kingdom, the realm of right relations in which all may find newness of life in Christ.

Clearly there are times for "holding" action. In spiritual warfare defense is necessary. We are instructed to watch as well as pray. But too often we are like the young fellow who loved tinkering with a somewhat antique automobile. He would work away, adjusting this part, changing that. A friend said, "Why don't you try it out on the road?" "Oh," replied the mechanic, "I don't want to go anywhere. I just like to hear the engine ticking over smoothly." But the living God created the Church and Christ loves the Church not so that it will "tick over smoothly," its machinery well oiled, with no skip in any cylinder. Christ loved the Church and gave himself for her that it might go somewhere— out into the midst of human beings in their need, their tragedy, their latent splendor. That "he might present it to himself without flaw or wrinkle or any such thing." The church which concentrates on its own safety will never achieve the purpose for which God brought it into being. Not a fire extinguisher, not a lotus blossom, not a contour chair for comfortable relaxation, is the central symbol of our holy faith, but a cross. And a cross is made of hardbeam and its grain is red. "He who has an ear, let him hear what the Spirit says to the churches."

President McCosh of Princeton University once remembered during prayers in chapel that he forgot to make an announcement, and he knew that students would rush out immediately after the benediction. So in his closing prayer he said: "And, O Lord, we ask thee to bless this great and noble institution of learning, its students here gathered, and not only these, but the faculty, especially the assistant professor of German, whose class will meet at half after nine this morning instead of ten as usual." But I need not wait until the prayer to say that the church has come to such a time *that we may realize increasingly her unity.* Can our Lord's prayer that all may be one be forever frustrated? Sufficient Calvinism lingers in our veins to assure us that with God what should be shall be. Only with all members of the orchestra playing under the baton of the Master of the music can we render worthily the New World Symphony of Christ. By loving the church, by helping the particular communion of the holy catholic church we love, and through which we serve to be true to herself and to her Lord, we shall help God to answer Christ's prayer.

Think not that in the king's palace—in the privileged position American churches occupy today—that we will escape the burdens of the Lord, nor silence his marching orders to his Church. For if we keep silent at such a time as this, relief and deliverance may come from another quarter; and we will perish through our own timidity, inertia, and pride. Nevertheless, who knows whether we have not come to God's kingdom for such a time as this?

51

# 7

# CAN WE BE CHRISTIANS WITH-OUT BEING CHURCHMEN?

*Harold A. Bosley*

Scripture: Acts 15:1-11, 22-29

THE PRESENT TREND IN CHURCH MEMBERSHIP IN THIS COUNTRY IS most reassuring to a student of our history. We have never had it so good, as the saying goes. Paul Douglas once estimated that at the end of the Colonial period in America—that is, in 1770 or 150 years after the Pilgrims came—less than five per cent of the population of America belonged to the church. One hundred and fifty years later—in 1920—nearly fifty per cent were church members. Today the proportion is nearer sixty per cent, and the pace of church membership is at least keeping pace with the increase in our population.

All this is reassuring, but one does not need to be a worry-head to be concerned about those who are outside the church. The parable of the good shepherd who sought out one lost sheep even though the ninety and nine were safely in the fold precludes any other attitude than that of concern.

## I

Let those of us who are churchmen make proper confession as we approach the question, "Can we be Christians without being churchmen?" If we were to reverse the terms in the question, it would be much easier to answer, wouldn't it? "Can we be churchmen without being Christians?" The answer to that, as all too frequently seen in our motives as well as our deeds, is "Yes." Even as it is possible for a man to "smile and smile and be a damned villain" we have it on good authority that it is possible for a man to cry, "Lord! Lord!" yet be far outside the fold of faithful followers. We have known many such people, and, in some of our moods, we are all as guilty as they of denying the spirit and the word of our Lord.

Bishop Arthur J. Moore delights in telling the story of a man in Georgia who came back to his home church after a dozen years spent in shady practices, in crime, and in jail. But he was all ready for the testimonial period, and when it came his turn he said: "I'm glad to be back in my own home church again. I want to tell you that while it's true I broke the law and beat my wife and served a term in jail, I want you to know, brethren, that I never lost my religion."

Actually, there is no argument over the correct answer to the question, "Can we be churchmen without being Christians?" The clouds of misunderstanding are certain to sweep in when we look at the query of the hour, "Can we be Christians without being churchmen?"

That question would not have been asked by anyone as recently as a hundred years ago. It never occurred even to the skeptic of earlier periods to claim that he could be a Christian and remain outside the church. When the great reformation movements were under way on the continent and in England, men did not move away from the Roman Catholic Church into no church; they moved into another church. Both Luther and Calvin were most explicit on that point. They denied that they ever left the Holy Catholic Church. They charged rather that Rome was subverting the true church—which they were trying to re-establish. To them as well as to a devout Romanist, it would have been a contradiction in terms for anyone to claim he could be a Christian and remain outside the church.

Not that Luther and Calvin had any illusions about the character of some people who get into the church. Calvin is appallingly abrupt about this: Churches do include "many hypocrites, who have nothing of Christ but the name and appearance; many persons ambitious, avaricious, envious, slanderous and dissolute in their lives." But granting this unhappy fact, Calvin never for a moment wavered in his insistence upon membership in the church. Putting it negatively, he said, "A departure from the church is a renunciation of God and Christ."

John Wesley was beginning to encounter a few who tried to separate loyalty to Christ from membership in the church, but he made short shrift of their plea: "There is no such thing as a solitary Christian."

But, though all our Luthers, Calvins, and Wesleys stand in serried ranks arrayed against us, many of our contemporaries continue to argue that it is possible to be a Christian without being a churchman. If you press them on the point, their answer usually takes one of two forms. First, they point out that there are hypocrites in the church—which means that there is no necessary connection between being a churchman and being a Christian. So far, so good—that is not only a lamentable fact, but it is an argument that must be granted. I have never known a churchman who doubted it. Then, they say that they believe in Jesus Christ and the Sermon on the Mount, and try to live by the Golden Rule. With that absolutely astounding claim, they usually sit back literally puffy with self-righteousness while we are faced with the choice of either admitting the claim and losing our case for the church, or challenging the claim and possibly losing a friend! But, friend or no, that claim must be looked into because it is hopelessly superficial and will not stand the test of serious question.

## II

Not a word in support of this can be found in the New Testament—that is a good point with which to begin. This is clearly so throughout the Gospels. Christ's call to men was always a call to enter in and to become an integral part of his followers, the new community. We need to proceed carefully at this point. He told them to enter into their closets and pray in secret; he told them "as a man thinketh in his heart, so is he." Leslie Stephens is right when he says that Jesus discovered the inner pole of morality. While no one has ever emphasized this inner pole of religious faith more than Jesus did, we ought never to forget that the first overt consequence of belief in Christ was to "leave all and follow him" in company with other believers. Bishop Charles Gore had the facts before him when he wrote: "There is nothing more central in the mind of Christ than that you can only love God in fellowship."

It was utterly unthinkable to the early Christians that one could be a Christian without belonging to the Christian fellowship. He had been called into the fellowship by Christ; he had been set apart from the world, but set apart by Christ. The early Christian was not called from a social unity into "splendid isolation"; he was called into "a household of faith." Paul's letters ring with dozens of exhortations which underscore this position. He urges his readers to bear one another's burdens, to let the needs of others be guides in their conduct, to strengthen the weak, to counsel the erring, to judge the quarrelsome, to conduct themselves in a respectable manner in their meetings, and to share in meeting the needs of food and shelter for the faithful. If ever you wonder about the earthy human nature of the early Christian community, read Rom. 16 again.

It is no surprise to learn that the church has always held to the New Testament line on this matter. Three forces, however, have been against her on this—and all three have grown to powerful maturity over the last two hundred years. First, there is the division within the church herself. No longer one church, but many different churches candidate for the right to interpret the Christian faith to men. The deep-seated differences between and among the churches have led many thoughtful people to the conclusion that any given church may not be a trustworthy guide.

A second fact drives an even more important wedge between Christianity and church membership; namely, the rise of individualism in the eighteenth century and the nineteenth century. Impatient of all authority, whether state or church, the individual sought to carve out a destiny under the sophomoric slogan:

> I am the master of my fate:
> I am the captain of my soul.[1]

[1] William Ernest Henley, "Invictus."

Robinson Crusoe was his unacknowledged hero—a self-sufficient man. This would have been news to Robinson Crusoe!

But more important than division and individualism is the feeling among many sincere people that the church is so hopelessly entangled in the *status quo,* so deeply involved in her own ecclesiastical life, that she is no longer able to carry out her prophetic function and witness. She is more intent on preserving and extending her life than losing it for the sake of the gospel, they think. Therefore, in order to be loyal to Christian teaching, they leave the church and devote themselves to special group efforts for economic and social justice and world peace.

## III

Actually of course the basic question in all this is a very ancient one: What does it mean to be a Christian? Jesus identified the great commandment as requiring love of God and love of neighbor. He commended the Golden Rule, "Whatsoever ye would that men should do to you, do ye even so to them." (Matt. 7:12.) He said, "Greater love hath no man than this, that a man lay down his life for his friends." (John 15:13.) He admonished the disciples, "By this shall all men know that ye are my disciples, if ye have love one to another." (John 13:35.)

To be a Christian—a follower of Jesus Christ—must mean to believe, to love, and to serve him. I do not see that it is possible for a person to do any one of these on his own, intra-dermally, as it were. They are deeply personal matters, to be sure. They touch the wellsprings of thought, feeling, and moral commitment, but they are as profoundly social as any conviction or enterprise could possibly be.

Take this matter of believing in Jesus Christ. Will even the most confirmed individualist among us claim that he can do this unassisted by anyone else? We would not even know of Christ had it not been for the church—the fellowship of the faithful who gathered around him as disciples and, later, around the disciples and the apostles as witnesses. The church alone has made it possible for us—any of us—to know about him, let alone believe in

56

him. Actually, all that we do in the church is a finger pointing at a fact—and Jesus Christ is that fact.

It is even more impossible to love him on our own, in splendid isolation; that is, if we are going to mean by love what he meant by it. He was not talking about an aesthetic yearning for beauty or truth when he spoke of love. He was talking about identifying himself with the object of love. To love God, as he meant it, was to identify himself with the will and the work of God in life, among people. To love one's neighbor, as he meant it, was to identify himself with the needs and the welfare of the neighbor, no matter who the neighbor was.

Love, as Jesus understood the term, is the very antithesis of a drawing apart from others. Rather it is the endless quest for an ever deeper relationship with them. It may begin, as one sly but discerning witness put it, with an effort "to love my crooked neighbor with all my crooked heart," but it cannot be content until men stretch hands of faith and love toward each other, saying, "We are one in Christ."

And how can we hope to serve him who gave himself for others unless we are willing to become one with all who love and seek to serve him? What does—what can—his final word to the disciples mean to the solitary individual? "Go ye therefore, and teach all nations." (Matt. 28:19.) That is the great commission. Can you frame a steadier call away from splendid isolationism than that?

## IV

I feel, therefore, that I must make this answer to the question, "Can we be Christians without being churchmen?" Yes, you probably can be a Christian without being a churchman, but you will be a pretty poor sort of Christian. You will be denying yourself some of the most important aids man has ever developed for the cultivation and the nurture of the Christian faith, and you will be denying your children such help as you yourself have had in becoming a Christian. You will be a poor sort of Christian yourself and your children won't even know the meaning of the word. That is rough talk I know, but no rougher than the facts require.

The first fact is this: Some kind of religious organization is essential to vital religion. Study the history of mankind with any care at all and you will discover this to be true. Vital religion—and I underscore the word "vital"—always expresses itself in and through some kind of historical and institutional tradition. But for that institution, the insights of faith would have perished rather than been perpetuated in the tradition and thereby made available to subsequent generations.

It is all right to say that religion is intensely personal, but we must not interpret that to mean that it is therefore private. It is concerned with our relationships with other people and with almighty God. Everything that has been important in art or science or literature has expressed itself in schools or traditions or institutions. By any manner of reckoning then, one of the tokens of the importance of religion—though not the only one—is this historic determination to insert itself as a social and institutional force in the unfolding life of mankind.

I am not now plugging for one particular kind of social organization when I speak of the church. In fact, I am of the opinion that over the nineteen hundred years of Christian history we have tried every conceivable form of social organization. What I am saying is that there has always been and must always be some kind of social form if we are to be able to receive, interpret, and perpetuate a tradition.

It is a matter of historical record that the church has done this with some measure of real success. It has done more than simply survive; it has grown and spread until it is one of the most important facts in human history. It has crossed all known borders and barriers that usually separate men from each other—clan, race, nation, culture. Though it has taken on—and cast off—many different social forms, the purpose of and in each one was the ancient goal of the disciples: *to preach Christ to all men.* The true marvel of the church is not the existence of so many different social forms of expression, but the continuing fidelity of each form to the single purpose of the Christian faith.

I repeat. This social organization has been and is "the carrier" of religious faith from one generation to another. Were it not for some such "carrier" there is no reason to think that the Christian faith would have survived the first generation of Christians. But it not only survived, it grew swiftly and began to bear fruit every-where.

I would urge a second fact upon those who think they can be a Christian without being a churchman: when you deliberately separate yourself from and stay outside the *influence* of the church you deny yourself the *fourfold ministry* of the church which has proved to be so effective in the cultivation and the nurture of the Christian faith over the years.

*First, there is the ministry of worship.* The church must both practice and cultivate the practice of the worship of God. This is the true foundation of her purpose, the true meaning of her life, and there can be no Christian faith without it. She is not an end in herself; she is the means to the end of receiving, inter-preting, and sharing the will of God. Our formal services of pub-lic worship do not serve their purpose unless they enable each participant to glimpse anew the glory of God which is trying to burst through the hymns, the scripture, the prayer, and the sermon. The first and fundamental movement in the life of the church is this mood of worship—sincere worship—of the living God.

The purpose of worship is simple: to galvanize men into action in the name, for the sake, and in the service of God. Worship is an earnest endeavor to confront God; it is man humbly but courageously trying to think God's thoughts after him; it is peo-ple like us trying to get some clear insight into the will of God in order that we may make God's will the will of our own life. It is a matter of simple historical record that the public worship of God has proved to be an indispensable instrument in the nurture of vital Christianity—and you who deny the church deny yourself this aid.

*You also deny yourself the ministry of education.* This is a necessary work for an institution which tries to bring nearly three millennia of human experiences to bear on our problems today. The Bible is the central document in our religious tradition, and only one who has never studied it seriously can think it a simple and easily understood and quite teachable book. It is no easy task to establish the relevance of biblical teachings to many of the problems we face today. Yet if the Bible is not to be treated as irrelevant, it must be brought into a vital relationship with everyday problems. To do this requires not only a knowledge of the Bible, but an acute understanding of the problems that are breaking the minds and the spirits of men today. This calls for the most careful kind of planning of a serious educational program in and through the ministry of the church. Even one who tries to live in splendid isolation is dependent upon the Christian scholars and teachers of the ages who have made possible the food on which he feasts alone in this private corner.

*You also deny yourself the ministry of fellowship which is fundamental to the church.* Historically, the church began in the homes of the faithful. The ministry of fellowship begun there continues to be an indispensable part of the work of the church. We are social beings. We were not meant to live alone but in communion with each other. When for any reason the bonds that bind us to any given group are severed, *instead of being freed, we more frequently feel lost.*

The church, to be true to her vision, must extend the mantle of fellowship to all men evenly. A class church, a race church, a national church are contradictions in terms, since they attempt to include some and exclude others of the human family from the fellowship of the church. The church must include all or else she is no Christian church. If a man really wants "to join the human race," he will want to do it in company with others.

*Finally, the man who tries to be a Christian without being a churchman would deny himself the ministry of social conscience which has been articulated in the church over the years.* Remember that it was a church conference that said:

The church is the champion of man against all that cheapens and degrades him; for the Gospel is the charter of man's dignity. The mission of the Church now as always is to proclaim and live out the Gospel by which alone men can be saved from sin and judgment, and the world from despair and self-destruction. . . . We must bring the teachings and the example of Christ into our everyday life. . . .

60

Nothing that is good in the sight of God should be outside the Church's interest.

## V

Intellectual integrity requires that we accept these facts at something like the face value of their meaning. And moral integrity requires that we ask where we fit into the life and the work of the church. As I address myself to those who may feel that they can be Christians without being churchmen, I want to make it clear that I am not urging them to accept a role of docile acquiescence in the church as she is. In fact, I most sincerely hope you will not do that. The church is far from perfect; she needs critics to help her understand the nature of her shortcomings. But remember this: the critic who counts most is the man who speaks from within.

If we are interested in the things that the church stands for, then moral integrity requires that we step up and take a position in that part or branch of the church that seems to be doing the best job of receiving and interpreting the tradition itself. It we feel that no existing form of the Christian church is doing this to our satisfaction, then we must either give up the religious insights that bear the name Christian or we must try to start a church of our own. To do other or less than that is to admit moral bankruptcy and the complete collapse of our religious faith.

Alfred North Whitehead once wrote: "Religion is what a man does with his solitariness." Insofar as this stresses the importance of personal feeling, belief, and commitment, it is true. But Christianity is more than what we do with our solitariness. It is what we do with our togetherness as well. Wesley's word is truer to known fact: "There is no such thing as a solitary Christian."

# 8

# NO SALVATION OUTSIDE THE CHURCH?

## *R. Brokhoff*

> And there is salvation in no one else, for there is
> no other name under heaven given among men by
> which we must be saved.—Acts 4:12 (R.S.V.)

> For where two or three are gathered in my name,
> there am I in the midst of them.—Matt. 18:20
> (R.S.V.)

*"Extra ecclesiam nulla salus."* THESE ARE THE FAMOUS WORDS OF
the third century bishop of Carthage, Cyprian. Translated, the
words say, "There is no salvation outside the church."

Does anyone agree with Cyprian? Seventy million Americans
do not agree, for if they did they would seek membership in the
church. These millions do not consider the church that important. They would not want to live in à community where there
was no church. They feel that the church is all right for those
who are socially inclined. But they would vigorously deny that
salvation depends upon membership in a local church.

Furthermore, millions who now belong to the church disagree
that there is no salvation outside the church. These Christians
claim confidently that church membership does not save the soul.
They remind us that there are people outside the church who are
just as good, if not better, than those inside the church. They point
to the hypocrites in the church.

Yet the church since the time of Cyprian has insisted that there
is no salvation outside the church. The Roman Catholic Church

with approximately 400 million souls and the Eastern Orthodox with 125 million members make this claim. Most Protestants agree that church membership is essential to salvation. Consider the statements of the two foremost leaders of the Reformation. Martin Luther wrote, "Outside the church is no truth, no Christ, no blessedness." John Calvin said, "No man can have God as his Father who has not the church as his Mother." We can go beyond Cyprian to the apostles and Christ. The theme of apostolic preaching is in Acts 4:12: "There is salvation in no one else, for there is no other name under heaven given among men by which we must be saved." To this we Christians unanimously agree. The name by which we are saved is Christ. What does it mean to believe in his name? The second text is: "Where two or three are gathered in my name, there am I in the midst of them." He who believes in the name of Christ is a Christian. When two or three believers come together, there is the church. Therefore, Christ is where the church is. To find Christ in order to believe in him we must go to the church. Luther put it this way: "Anyone who is to find Christ must first find the church."

For seventeen hundred years the church has reaffirmed Cyprian's words, "There is no salvation outside the church." A claim that has been believed for this length of time, accepted by millions of devout churchmen, must surely possess a valid truth. Why does the church persist in proclaiming such a tenet? Is it true, or does it represent only a means by which the church perpetuates itself?

## I

The first reasonable basis for this claim is found in the fact of experience—the church is the mother of our faith. We would all agree that we are saved by faith. "By grace are ye saved through faith" (Eph. 2:8), Paul wrote to the Ephesians. The apostles said, "Believe on the Lord Jesus Christ, and thou shalt be saved." (Acts 16:31.) They did not say, "Join the church, and you will be saved." But how does one secure this saving faith in Jesus Christ? Some acquire the faith through their home training. Others find faith by association with believing friends. Still others

receive faith by personal Bible study. But where did the home
and friends get the faith? Who produced the Bible? The home
and believing friends acquired their faith through the church.
The Bible, moreover, is the product of the church. Luther wrote:
"There would be no Bible, no sacraments without the church."
Faith does not come naturally to a person. We are not born with
it. It does not come by instinct or intuition. If it did, why do not
all men have saving faith in Christ?

Faith, then, is a gift of God. God through the Holy Spirit
arouses and creates in us saving faith in Christ as Savior. How does
the church enter into this birth of faith? The church has the word
of God and the sacraments through which the Holy Spirit comes
to the individual. Paul refers to "the sword of the Spirit, which
is the word of God" (Eph. 6:17). Faith comes by hearing the
word of God. The church teaches and preaches the word of God.
As men hear it with open minds and hearts, the Holy Spirit enters
and creates this saving faith. Luther taught: "I cannot by my own
reason or strength believe in Jesus Christ or come to him, but the
Holy Ghost has called me through the gospel."

The Holy Spirit also gives us faith through the sacraments of
the church, baptism and the Lord's Supper. This is possible because a sacrament is the word of God accompanied by a physical
sign such as water. When a man is baptized he receives the gift
of the Holy Spirit as Jesus did when he was baptized in the Jordan.
Each time we receive the Lord's Supper the Holy Spirit is renewed in us.

Is the church essential to salvation? It is a necessary means of
grace. A man is saved by faith in Christ. This faith is a gift of the
Holy Spirit who is received through the word of God, the textbook
of the church, and the sacraments which are necessary for that
faith which saves the soul. The church then is the mother of our
faith. As a mother is necessary for the birth of a child, the church
is necessary for salvation.

## II

Secondly, "there is no salvation outside the church" because
the church is the communion of saints, the fellowship of believers

in Christ. Thus far we have agreed that we are saved by faith in Christ and that faith is a gift of the Holy Spirit received through the church's means of grace, the Word and sacraments. To have faith then is to have the Holy Spirit. If the Spirit is possessed, believers will be drawn together. The Holy Spirit is a centrifugal force that attracts believers into churches. The power of the Spirit is a divine magnet which draws all men to Christ and to each other. The Spirit gathers men into congregations. This helps us to understand that the church is a divine creation through the Holy Spirit. Christians are together because of the work of God. The church is not a human club or an association for mutual benefit. The church is of God, called by God, gathered by God for divine purposes. This constitutes the value of the church, its importance, and its permanence.

"Why can't I be a Christian without joining the church?" The answer is that a Christian would be in the church. The Holy Spirit makes a man a Christian, and if he is a Christian through the work of the Holy Spirit, that same spirit draws him to other Christians in the church. An individual Christian is no Christian at all. There is no solitary Christian. Christianity has always been a fellowship in Christ. Refusal to join the church on the claim that a man can be a Christian outside the church is the confession of a grave sin. This refusal usually results from a sense of self-sufficiency, independence, and exclusiveness. These are manifestations of man's worst sin, pride.

It is not therefore surprising that true Christians through the centuries have always been in the church. If ever a man could have felt the church to be unnecessary, he was Jesus. Yet he did not stay away from the "church" of his day. It was his custom to go to the synagogue on the Sabbath, and he made many trips to the temple. As a baby he was circumcised and became a part of the Jewish nation, the people of God. Jesus' religion grew out of the Jewish faith. The New Testament is the fulfillment of the Old. The first Christians were Jews. Even after the resurrection, they continued to worship in the temple and used the traditional prayers. Christianity was not a separatist movement. It was the natural outgrowth of new life and spirit brought by Christ. Since the time of Christ, to be in Christ has meant to be in the church.

Is this fellowship essential for salvation? It is in the sense that fellowship with Christians in the church retains that saving faith in Christ. To try to keep the faith by living apart from fellow Christians is just about impossible, because the world is too strong for us. The insidious temptations of the world unite to destroy our faith in spiritual matters. A Christian needs the church to keep his faith. It is common for a man who stops attending church to feel a loss of faith. One or two absences may not make much difference, but as the absences continue a man slowly and painlessly loses his faith. A Sunday-school superintendent went to see a man who was no longer attending. As they were discussing the problem before the fireplace, the superintendent set apart one of the logs. It soon stopped burning, although the other logs kept blazing. The absentee replied: "I see exactly what you mean. You need not say another word. I will be back next Sunday." Are we able to see the truth just as clearly and forcefully?

The fellowship of the church is necessary, furthermore, to nourish our faith in Christ. Faith is contagious. The faith of others helps our faith to grow and mature. When our faith falters or is weak, we need to go to church where the strong faith of fellow members encourages and inspires our faith. When we join in singing the hymns of faith, our faith is strengthened. When we see how men have conquered through their faith, we know we can do the same. As we see men of prominence in the community bend their knees in humility and confession, we are inspired to make a true confession of our sins. Moreover, it is in the fellowship of Christians that we hear the word of God preached and taught and the sacraments administered. These feed our souls and faith is increased.

How necessary is the Church for salvation? How necessary is the vine to the branch? Apart from the vine, the branch withers and dies. The church is the body of Christ, the vine. The individual Christian is a branch. When a man accepts Christ, he is engrafted into the vine from which he receives life and strength. To be a Christian means to have fellowship with Christ, and to have fellowship with Christ means to share the fellowship of believers which is the church.

## III

Thirdly, "there is no salvation outside the church" because the church is the body of Christ. We agreed that we are saved by faith in Christ. Who has this faith? Do we agree with James that faith without works is dead? Faith, to be true faith, means obedience. To believe in Christ means to obey a command like "Go ye therefore, and teach all nations, baptizing them" (Matt. 28:19). To baptize, a man must first be baptized. To be baptized means to be initiated into the body of Christ, the church. He who claims to believe in Christ and refuses to be baptized and join the church does not have true faith.

To express this faith there must be a means of expression. How can a spirit express itself without a body? On earth there is no disembodied spirit. A body is essential to the spirit's existence on earth. This faith of ours needs a body by which to express itself. That body is the church which Paul describes as the body of Christ. The church then is the extension of the Incarnation. The church is the contemporary presence of Christ in our midst. Through the church Christ today speaks and teaches and heals.

We need the church as a body through which we can express our faith. "Why can't we serve Christ without belonging to the church?" There is much the Christian can do outside the church. He has personal virtues to develop. He can love his neighbor in a personal way. He can witness for Christ at the office or in the factory. But a man cannot discharge his full responsibility apart from the church. He needs the church to obey the commands of Christ. Through the church the individual Christian can do things he could not do alone. How can he as one individual win the world for Christ? Can he go out as a single missionary? Through the church he can do his part in commissioning missionaries. A Christian is to win the country for Christ by planting missions. He needs the church to support mission pastors, build parsonages and chapels, provide literature and equipment. Because individual Christians work together, one church in America established fifteen hundred mission churches in five years. "Do good unto all men" is the Christian's command. How can one answer the needs of ten million refugees for example? Yet one church since World War II raised $45 million for physical and spiritual rehabilitation of dispossessed people and sent an additional $48 million worth of food, clothing, and medicine to the needy throughout the world. And what shall we say about the Christian's responsibility to provide Christian education and care of the sick, aged, and orphaned? The individual needs the church to provide the necessary institutions.

As a single Christian needs the church as a body through which to express his faith, Christ needs the church to cleanse the Christian from his sin. He does this through the word of the gospel. His word cleanses the soul: "Ye are clean through the word I have spoken unto you" (John 15:3). In the sacraments of the church, Christ cleanses us from sin. When he passed the cup of wine, he said it was his blood "for the remission of sins" (Matt. 26:28). When we go to church regularly and hear the Word and receive the sacraments, our souls are cleansed. We may not be able to contain all the truth we hear, but the truth and grace, passing through our minds and hearts, cleanses us.

Christ uses the church as his body also to empower us to live lives worthy of him. The Holy Spirit comes to us through the Word and sacraments, and enables us to live better lives to his glory. Consequently, the church contains the best people on earth. Facts prove it! Several years ago the FBI reported that only five per cent of our crime can be traced to church people, but 95 per cent of America's crime is committed by the forty per cent of the non-churched population. What kind of people have the best personalities? In a nationwide personality test, it was found that those with the best personalities go to Sunday school or belong to a religious organization. In this land where more than one thousand divorces are granted daily, non-churched homes break up three times as often as Christian homes. These facts should not be surprising. Christ does make a difference in life.

"There is no salvation outside the church," though a true statement, may give a false sense of spiritual security. Not everyone in the church is saved. Some join the church without saving faith or lose their faith while members. On the other hand, those who are saved are in the church. Therefore, join the church, love the church, serve the church, for "there is no salvation outside the church"—*"Extra ecclesiam nulla salus."*

# 9

# BE AN INTELLIGENT PROTESTANT

*Clifford Ansgar Nelson*

> Always be prepared to make a defense to any one
> who calls you to account for the hope that is in you,
> yet do it with gentleness and reverence.—I Pet. 3:15
> (R.S.V.)

ON OCTOBER 31ST OF THIS YEAR IT WILL BE MORE THAN 440 YEARS
since Martin Luther posted his ninety-five theses and started the
movement which is known as the Protestant Reformation. Little
did he think on that fateful day that what he was doing would
be counted as the beginning of a new era in the life of religion.
No one was more surprised than he to discover that the academic
discussion that was started according to the pattern of that day
would be remembered and celebrated across the centuries as a
moment of release and liberation for the human spirit. Long
afterward he said: "Had I known in advance, God would have
been put to great trouble to bring me to do it." Concerning the
decisive moment of history that transpired at the Diet of Worms
in 1521 he wrote: "Truly God can drive one mad. I do not know
whether now I could have been so daring." But like Columbus
a few decades earlier, he discovered a whole new world. It was
the discovery of the inner soul of man in relation to God.

Today in our country it does not take great courage or audacity
to be a Protestant. Once it meant social ostracism and persecution,
but now too frequently Protestantism is the designation for a sort
of miscellaneous, conventional, easygoing kind of religion that
lacks dynamic and conscious conviction.

There is need therefore for Protestants to be aware of their religious heritage and their continuing responsibility to guard the precious ideals that inspired the Reformation and that continue to inspire our Western world. For too many the designation Protestant means something negative. It can easily signify that one is against something. But originally to be a Protestant was to be a witness of a great faith and conviction. It derives from the primary meaning of the word *protestari* which means to make an affirmation, to express a conviction, to make an avowal of a faith, to witness to a great reality of truth.

Each of us needs to know intelligently why we are Protestants. We need to be able to give an intelligent defense of the hope and the faith that we have, and to do it without intolerance or rancor, minus any bigotry or bitterness. It is our task in America to live side by side with those whose faith is not our own, and we need to know and understand one another in appreciation and friendly neighborliness. And that means to know where we stand in regard to our own faith. We need to know what it is that makes our cultural and religious patterns different from those of our Roman Catholic friends. We need to be aware of where we are alike in our common tradition of the Christian faith, but also where we differ. We need to be informed of the historical and profound religious differences that separate us so that we may be aware of the continuing task that must inspire us in our carrying out of the implications of the Protestant faith.

To that end let us look at some of the areas where we need to keep clear our witness to the quality of democracy in religion, which is the atmosphere of the Protestant faith.

## I

A Protestant must know what constitutes the faith which he professes. It is at this point where many are confused. Let us be grateful to acknowledge the many places where we are at one with our Roman Catholic brethren. We, together with them, freely acknowledge the three common ecumenical creeds as our own. The Apostles' Creed, the Nicene Creed, and the Athanasian Creed we hold in common. We are at one as the bearers of the great Judeo-Christian tradition of our religious heritage. We acknowledge the same sovereign creator, God, the same divine Son of God, Savior Redeemer of the world. We breathe the same blessed prayer of our Lord when we speak to our Father who art in heaven. We cherish the same ideals of moral integrity and the same hope of life everlasting.

We too are catholics. In the words of our common creed we believe in one holy, catholic, and apostolic church. We are glad to be known as evangelical catholics, but we are equally determined not to be known as Roman. For it is at this point where we repudiate the leadership of the church of Rome.

Instead we would want to lay stress on the oneness of all Christians in all the world who profess the name of Christ and hold him to be the Savior of the world. We resent propaganda which tries to make our Protestant church a community founded in the sixteenth century. The Protestant Reformation sought nothing quite so much as to push back across the centuries to discover anew and afresh the apostolic and New Testament character of the church. We want to be true to the gospel of Christ and the church which he founded. No excommunication from Rome could ever sever the reformers from that church where Christ is the Lord and true believers confess his name.

There are many things that I admire about Roman Catholics. Their concern for religious education, their zeal for missions, their earnestness about a life of prayer, their discipline of regular attendance at worship, their desire for saintliness and scholarship—all these are admirable and worthy of that great communion. But the narrow sectarianism of a church that wants to teach its people that they are the only true church of Christ, the domineering exclusiveness that refuses to acknowledge other Christians as being members of a true and valid fellowship of believers in Jesus Christ—that I regret. When the ministry of all other churches is counted as not having a valid ministry, and the sacraments of all other churches as not being proper and valid in their efficacy before God, then I protest.

It is at this place where democracy in religion and true understanding among fellow countrymen calls for discussion and mutual consultation. But this has become increasingly impossible. I regret exceedingly that the Roman leadership has refused to permit her priests and leaders to sit down at the conference table to talk frankly with responsible leaders about their differences. Recently the World Council of Churches and the Lutheran World Federation have asked that in a worthy and responsible way there shall be a meeting of theologians and church leaders on high levels for common discussion of our mutual concern for the religious life of the age in which we live. Our wrestling with the powers of evil and darkness is one and the same in this desperate generation that hangs on the brink between life and death. The response of Rome has thus far been silence or repudiation of the idea. Let us pray and hope that there will still come an answer to a sincere and honest request for conference and deliberation.

## II

A Protestant must know the church of which he is a member. We Protestants believe in the church, and we believe in Christ as the sole head of that church. From him alone do we take our marching orders. That church is an integral part of Christ's way of salvation. In it the Holy Spirit lives and moves and brings forth the truth that was once and for all given to the saints. In it we are a great family gathered from all nations, in communion with believers in Christ in all ages, and we are united under the sovereignty and lordship of Jesus Christ alone. That is our faith with regard to the church which is the body of Christ.

## III

A Protestant must know the central place of the Bible in all faiths. All the great communions of non-Roman Christendom are united on the great affirmation of the Reformation that the Bible is the sufficient and only rule of faith and life. Actually the Reformation began there. We cannot forget the epoch making answer of Martin Luther at the Diet of Worms when he was asked to recant the writings that were under question. His answer was to the effect that he would be ready to take back all that he had written if it could be proved by the scriptures and good reason that he had erred, for "My conscience is captive to the Word of

God." That is a golden Protestant affirmation. An intelligent Protestant today will understand what it means to have one's conscience bound to the word of God alone, for therein lies real freedom. God's word can never lead any man astray. It alone offers freedom of thought and life. Therein lies the truth that can make us free indeed.

The Protestant movement has been willing to run the risk of urging every Christian to know and to love and to read his Bible. That is democracy in religion. The Bible must not be simply the preoccupation of the learned doctors and interpreters under the sole imprimatur of the ecclesiastical authorities. The Bible is the book for the plain man who is hungry for God. Therein he will find the way to Christ and the path of life and salvation. That book is a forward looking book. Inspired through the Holy Spirit of God by prophets and evangelists and apostles, it still is a lamp unto our feet and the light upon all our pathway. And that inspiration will constantly lead us to reform and keep alive the faith which constantly kindles new life and inspiration.

## IV

The Protestant will know the way of access to God. Luther had sought peace with God by every known means at his disposal. The story of his tortuous search through penance and fasting, through alms and vigils, is well known. But in his search of the scripture it became clear to him, almost as though it were a fresh discovery, that there was no other way to find peace with God than through faith in the atoning Christ. It was when he found the Pauline way of the New Testament that he saw how God justifies the sinner. It was when looking at Rom. 1:16-17 that he seemed to feel that the very gates of paradise were swinging open for his soul; and he found a release and a joy that he proclaimed as the central teaching of all Christianity. This was God's way. This was the Biblical faith. "He who through faith is righteous shall live." (Rom. 1:17 R.S.V.)

That is the kind of release and salvation we all need. Modern psychology talks of this kind of release in different language, to be sure, but with an insight into something profound in our religious faith. All of us want to be acceptable to ourselves, to others, and to God. But how? The religious way of putting it is that God makes us acceptable, not by our own goodness or our own merits, but through the faith which we put in Christ. Then, even though I am still a sinner, I am justified by that faith, and God covers me with the robe of Christ's righteousness so that I am received and acceptable to God. Then I can accept myself, and I can have confidence in my life before men. And because I am thus made acceptable, even though I will never be perfect enough, I will eagerly and gladly try to make my life an answer of gratitude for God's great love and peace. I will seek to make myself what God wants me to be.

V

The Protestant will find joy in his worship of God. We Protestants do not realize what a shock Luther administered to his world when he made innovations in the ancient liturgical pattern of his church. We take our Protestant worship for granted. But when Luther's nationalism and patriotism were stirred he began thinking that there was nothing so sacrosanct about the classic and beautiful Latin language of the church that it must be perpetuated forever in Christian worship. It was a true instinct that he had when he began, cautiously at first, to render the Mass into the language of the people. Why should we not talk to God in the language that we use in our daily speech? It was democracy in religion again, and we Protestants are glad for a worship that is conducted in our own vernacular, and for sacred hymns and the ancient chants of the worship of the church in our own language. We love the ancient Gregorian melodies and the classic forms of worship of our churches, but it is a sign of our Protestantism that all worshipers join in them together. In the Roman Mass the hymn book is never used by the people. The chants and liturgical hymns are a domain of the choir and the priest. An intelligent Protestant will join in the liturgy and hymnody of his church with hearty joy.

The atmosphere of worship in the Roman Church is one of

solemn and dramatic beauty. Who of us, when we have visited, has not thrilled at the color and awe and reverence of the Mass? But think for a moment. The meaning of the celebration of the Mass is the constant re-enacting of the sacrificial drama of salvation. The lights and the vestments, the incense and the altar bell, the worshiping congregation watching in prayer as the dramatic service is enacted—all of this is impressive. The remembrance of the story of salvation must forever be told and dramatized, although we do not feel that the sufficient sacrifice of Calvary needs to be re-enacted. It was once and for all made on the hill of the cross.

But Protestant worship introduced another mood and atmosphere of worship. Luther put it beautifully when he defined worship as the place where "we may come together to act and hear God's word; that our dear Lord may speak to us through His holy Word; that we in turn may speak to Him through prayer and songs of praise." It is the place where we hear God speak and where we speak to him. That is not drama so much as dialogue. It is the interplay and rhythm of the speech of God to man and man to God. To hear God's word in the liturgy, in the sermon, in the reading of scripture, and to answer with confession of sin and faith and the response of praise and prayer—that is worship. An intelligent Protestant will not be passive in worship. He is not in church to enjoy the music and the preacher. He is there to hear God speak and then to speak with God in the full response of his heart.

## VI

A Protestant will understand the true priesthood of all believers. That means something dynamic for every believer. It means that every believer is called to a sacred ministry. The distinction that obtained in medieval times between the secular and religious task is an untrue distinction. If a man believes in Christ, his vocation, his calling, his daily work will be a sacred and holy task. Just as a minister is ordained to the task of preaching and to administering the sacraments, so the layman is ordained to fulfill his holy task of prayer and intercession, and of doing an honest job in the place where he is at work. Whether he be a laborer or a prime minister, whether he be a banker or a lawyer, a housewife or a secretary, a teacher or a businessman, all labor ranks the same with God. Luther dusted off the religious word "vocation" and insisted that when there is faith in Christ, all tasks are holy and we are fellow workers with God in bringing the radiance of eternity into the daily round.

Here is another form of democracy in religion which is the glory of the Reformation and which must be asserted in our world which has so greatly lost this sense of holiness in the daily task. This gives a dignity and worth to the common man. It was in this kind of belief in the sacredness of a man's own worth that our pilgrim fathers cradled their political democracy in the town meeting where the word of each man had meaning because a man was of worth to God. This has reared a democratic trust in the common mind which we must not lose. I love the sound of an old epitaph in a churchyard in England that reads: "To Thomas Cobb, who mended shoes in this village for 40 years to the glory of God." That is a great tribute. The believer is a priest before God. His life of faith is as holy as that of any man of God in the pulpit or at the altar. His task is a teamwork with all believers in serving the Master of us all.

This is our witness. And this is the continuing task of witness and service which Protestant Christians must carry on in our world. This is the constant reformation which must continue to cleanse and democratize and unify the church of Christ in the whole world. We must continue to live in the spirit of the Reformation and continually rediscover afresh the truths that were so dearly bought and have been held through these centuries. We must constantly test our standards and our actions by the life and the words of Jesus who promised that the spirit of God would constantly reveal the truth in every fresh disclosure to his children.

Of this faith we Protestants are unashamed. We recognize it as the gospel which has come to us from our Lord. We will shun all hatred and bigotry and seek to live in peace with those of another church or faith, without prejudice. Long ago, John Wesley wrote, "I entreat you, be a real Protestant." That means to be an intelligent believer who knows the Protestant faith and rejoices in it, who witnesses to it "with gentleness and reverence."

# III

*Evangelism and World Outreach*

# THE HORIZONS OF EVANGELISM

*Albert Edward Day*

> The Spirit of the Lord is upon me, because he has
> anointed me to preach good news to the poor. He
> has sent me to proclaim release to the captives and
> recovering of sight to the blind, to set at liberty those
> who are oppressed.—Luke 4:18 (R.S.V.)

CHRISTINE ARNOTHY, WHEN ONLY FIFTEEN YEARS OF AGE, SHARED
the plight of civilians who hid in a cellar in Budapest, waiting
out the battle between Germans and Russians in hunger, thirst,
and terror. At long last the Germans withdrew, leaving one of
their wounded soldiers at the cellar's entrance. Should they give
him aid or let him die? On the human level, after what they had
suffered, there were strong arguments why he should die. "Suddenly," recalled the girl many years after, "I had the impression
that the ruins over our heads had ceased to exist and that, from
heaven, God was watching to see how we were going to pass
through this ordeal. . . . Would we consider only a uniform and
allow a human life to flow away, drop by drop under our eyes?"
When anybody becomes aware of God and begins to see people
and situations as God sees them, it makes a tremendous difference.
It did in that cellar. The soldier was not left to die!

"The Spirit of the Lord is upon me." Jesus was not only God-
conscious but God-possessed! He saw people—the poor, the en-
slaved, the blind, and the oppressed—as God saw them. He felt
for them as God felt. He dedicated himself to do for them what
God would do. Hence came the noblest evangelism in history.
Name all the evangelists in both Catholic and Protestant tradi-

tion, and when you have recognized their worth you still must say, "No mortal can compare with him among the sons of men."

We ought to be chary of any evangelism that, in manner, method, or spirit, contradicts what Christ said or did. We ought not to be content with any that omits what he said and did.

## I

The evangelism of Christ had a wide horizon. Its concern was with all classes. It had a message for the rich and the poor, the cultured and the uncouth, the exploiter and the exploited, the conqueror and the conquered. The common people heard him gladly, but the uncommon people could not ignore him. The rulers did not follow him up and down the dusty roads of Galilee; but, seated on their political or ecclesiastical thrones, they knew that he meant them and confronted them with an inescapable choice. The ruled knew, whether they obeyed or rebelled against their political and ecclesiastical sovereigns, that there was a higher sovereignty overarching their often pitiful lives. More important than the taxes they paid to Caesar was the question as to whether they would give their hearts to this Man in their midst.

It was an evangelism for all ages. "Youth for Christ" did not begin in Philadelphia or New York, but across the sea when some self-important adults tried to steer children away from Jesus, and he reached out his arms and bade them come. Hobbling age also felt the spell of his message and responded.

It was an evangelism for all areas of life. It included in its concern what men did when they "devoured" a widow's house, as well as when they went into the house of God to offer their "devotions." It not only taught men to pray with reverence, but rebuked them when their rapacity preyed upon their fellows. No stronger words were ever spoken about justice than were incorporated in his memorable utterance:

Woe to you, scribes and Pharisees, hypocrites! for you tithe mint and dill and cummin, and have neglected the weightier matters of the law, justice and mercy and faith; these you ought to have done, without neglecting the others. (Matt. 23:23 R.S.V.)

82

Who that has read it can ever forget his story of the unjust judge and his arresting question, "And will not God vindicate his elect, who cry to him day and night? Will he delay long over them?" (Luke 18:7). No fair interpretation can evade the social implications of such langauge. To assume that Jesus was concerned with souls only, and not with systems and practices which tortured and damned souls, is to reveal a blindness that refuses to see what is obvious to anyone who will open the eyes of his mind.

It was an evangelism of bread and butter as well as of the spirit. "Give ye them to eat." (Matt. 14:16.) It was concerned with men's bodies, with their aches and pains as well as with their aspirations and prayers. "So his fame spread throughout all Syria, and they brought him all the sick, those afflicted with various diseases and pains, demoniacs, epileptics, and paralytics, and he healed them." (Matt. 4:24 R.S.V.) It spoke to men's minds with a clarity and insight that centuries has not dimmed. It spoke to men's hearts with warmth and understanding. The human heart was never in such safe hands as when Jesus was near. It spoke to men's wills; it was not an orgy of emotionalism nor a futile sentimentalism, but a pattern and preparation for action: "This do, and thou shalt live" (Luke 10:28).

Here are the horizons of a truly Christian evangelism! By Christ are we in this confused and confusing era summoned to a new breadth of concern and appeal.

Protestantism is frightfully in danger of becoming a middle-class church. I for one am glad it at least is that; otherwise I could not be in it. But it must become very much more. Both the "up-and-outs" and the "down-and-outs" need the gospel. Some of the loneliest and most wretched people in the world are in the upper income brackets, and for the most part we are not reaching them. Sometimes we seem not to care for them; sometimes we think them beyond the reach of our message. When we are in their presence our tongues are palsied. We talk about everything else but Christ. We are overawed by the glamor of the external, and fail to sense the internal famines from which they suffer. What is worse, we have no intelligent strategy for reaching them. In many respects, our Roman Catholic friends are much wiser. They have not abandoned people of wealth and position. Nor are they leaving them to the chance influence of some neighboring priest. But with skill, astuteness, and finesse they have evolved a strategy to capture the leadership of America. They have had some very conspicuous results. It is time we woke up, not to unholy rivalry, but to an equally Christian concern.

At the other end of the social scale we also need a vastly greater sense of responsibility and opportunity. Several years ago in California there was an invasion of what men called somewhat scornfully the "Oakies" and the "Arkies." People whom John Steinbeck lifted into public notice in *The Grapes of Wrath*, humble folk, often illiterate, were drawn westward by the hope of escaping, from dust bowls and the seemingly hopeless poverties of exhausted farms, to the salubrious climate and fertilities of the Golden Gate. They moved into the neighborhoods of our churches, but our services scarcely touched them. Some preachers were not disturbed by the fact. They said: "These migrants are not our kind. Our message and method do not appeal to them. Only 'Holy Rollerism' can reach them." Other preachers asked anxiously, "What can we do to save these people?" Once our churches knew the answer and gave it. Is it that we do not know the answer now? Or are we not willing to extend ourselves enough to give it?

The story in rural areas and congested urban communities is often little different. Too frequently our method has been flight rather than quest. We have not evangelized; we have evaporated and disappeared. To be sure, we have called it by other names—"consolidation" or "relocation"—but a relocation that takes us away from the squalor and poverty and ignorance of any of God's children is dislocation, and consolidation that severs our redemptive links with sinful, sorrowing, suffering humanity means consternation in heaven, whatever consent it wins in ecclesiastical councils on earth.

Unless we are as broad as human need, we are too narrow for Christ. Paul was sure of that when he wrote: "To the weak I became weak, that I might win the weak. I have become all things to all men, that I might by all means save some" (I Cor.

9:22 R.S.V.). There was no liturgical "starch" in the hem of Christ's garment! A truly Christian church is one with room enough for all sorts of temperament and flexible enough to meet the psychological needs arising out of the varying cultural backgrounds of the people around it. Classical music is not the only medium through which the gospel may sing its way into the hearts of men. Nor is the lingo of theology or philosophy the only path over which Christ may walk to the sinner's door! Stately music is not the only sacred music. Many of us prefer it to the "singspiration" that is in vogue in many places, just as we prefer the philosophical and theological discourse to the storybook, story-sermon type of utterance. But songs the people can sing and language they can understand have in many situations an evangelical effectiveness that is truly sacred.

A letter came to my desk not long ago that is very relevant here. It was from a woman of genuine culture whose heart is greatly burdened for the masses. She wrote mournfully: "In my humble opinion, many leaders, including pastors and teachers, are not only remote—they are insulated from reality." She suggests that we forego some institutes and retreats and get a job in a factory, mine, filling station or department store, where the people are poor and of the more untutored type, and work for at least a month. She adds, "We can talk about needs, we can make plans, we can guess; but all that is no substitute for knowing." Too often we do not know. We do not really think and feel with the masses and so they cannot think and feel with us. How many labor leaders or laboring men and women were delegates to the recent General Conference of The Methodist Church or the General Assembly of the Presbyterian Church, for example? How many sit on our official boards or commissions? Our duty is not to agree with them always, any more than it is to agree with the chamber of commerce or the American Legion. But it should be our passion to understand them and help them to understand us and the significance of our Christ for their work and their love and their dreams.

In many places we must reorient ourselves to youth. That does not imply compromise with teen-age fantasies and furies. They will only despise us if we do that. It does mean that youth is alive, full of energy, hungry for action; has feeling for drama and capacity for dreams, and wants to be challenged with the difficult and dangerous. Nice little Sunday evening programs, prepared according to some desk man's idea of what constitutes a "worship service," leave them bored. Across the country youth have come to us, asking not about organization, program-making, and discussion groups; but how to pray, how to find God, how to have conscious comradeship with Christ, how to live like Christ in an unchristian world. They do not want easy answers. They want real answers. Again and again we tell these romantic youth that there is no love like the love of Christ, no life like an all out life for him, no way to God except by the Cross on which the world is crucified to them and they to the world. We tell them that there is no hope for this jittery world, except as the Spirit of Christ gets into business, and politics, and international relations via personalities wholly dedicated to Christ. Again and again we dare them to die in order that they might live, and they accept the challenge! Youth is within the life-making outreach of Christ's love and grace. Christ is their hearts' desire, though often they do not know it until he is interpreted to them and they are interpreted to themselves. Is our evangelism broad enough for that?

## II

If we are to have the breadth of Christ, many of us must achieve a greater conception of Christ's relevance to every area where men live and toil. Certainly we should by this time have dismissed the hackneyed antithesis between the individual and the social gospel. The gospel begins with the individual, his sins and his need of a Savior, his self-centeredness, and his need of deliverance from self. Until something happens to him, all our efforts toward economic justice, decency, and world peace will fail. The gospel begins with the individual, but does not end there. Any religious experience which truly saves a man will transform his social relationships. If what has happened to him does not make him a better husband, a more conscientious citizen, a more dependable employee, a better mayor, judge, legislator, or administrator, then he has not been "saved." He has only been emotionalized. Our fathers preached to men purity, justice, honesty, and love. We need to inquire what these virtues really involve in the context of an industrial society, and make an ethic relevant to such a society. Otherwise, we shall have an evangelism that is irrelevant and ineffective. Instead of life-shaking conviction of sin, we shall have only shallow regret. Instead of life-changing repentance, we shall have only fleeting sorrow for insignificant blunders. Instead of life-making regeneration and sanctification, we shall have only slight modifications of personal behavior. We make Christians only when we Christianize life in its entirety.

Is our evangelism concerned enough with men's bodies? A large part of the ministry of Jesus was devoted to the healing of the sick. Why have we left spiritual healing to quacks and exploiters and to those whose fumbling philosophy adulterates the truth about the human body with destructive illusions about the human soul? This minister belongs to a seminar composed of physicians, psychiatrists, and psychosomatic therapists, who are profoundly interested in our adventures in this field. Some of them employ the techniques of spiritual healing in their private practice. All of them are friendly and co-operative. Doctor Christopher Woodward of London writes of his relations with his patients:

> We invariably pray together and I often wish that some priests and doctors could see what happens. I am sure that we see better results than a doctor could possibly hope for who relied purely on medical and scientific knowledge.

Some of the most thrilling hours in our seminars have been those when doctors have witnessed to literally miraculous healings that have taken place as they have prayed for patients for whom apparently there was not hope. Karl Heim, a theologian who is thoroughly at home in the world of modern physics, writing in *The Transformation of the Scientific World View*, says:

> Now at last we are able to break free from the overweening power of [the] causal-mechanical picture of nature, which works on suffering

87

people like a "bad suggestion," and hinders them from bringing their spiritual power into action against the disease.[1]

Science is beginning to catch up with Jesus in his understanding of the role of faith, hope, and love in the cure of disease and the maintenance of health. But we who are supposed to be followers of Jesus are still following him afar off. We say prayers for the sick, but we do not really expect anybody to get well because of our intercession. We seldom hold services for the sick in which we prepare them to receive spiritual healing.

## III

Is our evangelism concerned enough with men's minds? Is it intelligent and intelligible? Do we give men reasons, or do be belabor them with exhortations or emotionalize them with illustrations? Theology alone cannot save. But the man who has not some kind of theology will not stay saved very long. Secularism, humanism, naturalism—the inevitables of life—will soon scuttle his Godward dedications and expectations. Beliefs are not synonymous with saving faith, but a faith with no intelligible beliefs will degenerate into fanaticism or disintegrate into a chronic skepticism. The neglect of the teaching function in evangelism is a major crime against the gospel of the Christian church, filled with people who do not know what they believe about the great essentials. They do not know because we have not dealt honestly and lovingly with their minds. A chaplain once said to me, "I have tried to help scores of dying men after bloody engagements, but many of our church boys were as bad off as those who had never gone to church." Our evangelism had brought these boys into church, but had not given them clear conviction to which they could cling and by which they could be steadied as the last darkness crept in upon them! Outside the church multitudes are not won for Christ because our intellectual anachronisms have come between them and Christ. They have not seen him who is the Truth because of the obscurantisms and confusions of our

[1] (New York: Harper & Brothers, 1953), p. 184.

preaching. They know some of the things we say are not so. They doubt if the rest is. They cannot believe in Christ because they do not believe in us, in our integrity of mind. His insights are hidden behind our absurdities and our inanities.

How much heart is there in our evangelism? I do not mean how many "tear-jerkers" get into our preaching, nor how expertly do we angle for a laugh, nor how deliberately or skillfully do we play for an emotional response. Rather, do I mean is there warmth—the warmth of concern, pity, understanding, and love? Do people go away from our services feeling that we really care? Do they sense in us an awareness of their plight and an inner agony about it? Are our sermons opportunities for the display of logic, eloquence, and power over congregations? Or are they the outreach of a loving heart, greatly awed by the adventure of life and grieved for those who are making it a misadventure? Only hearts can speak to hearts and save hearts. Can we be trusted to strike no false notes in the gamut of human emotions, to cultivate no shallow sentimentalisms about God and life, to administer no opiates, to promote no complacencies? Do we link emotion with reality? Do we wound where wounds are necessary to awaken and purge? Do we offer solace only where the truth can solace? Do we arouse only emotions that will lead to salutary action?

How truly do we speak to men's wills? Do we give them a pattern for action and a preparation for it? Nothing less can satisfy men, for they are creatures of action. Nels Ferré has epitomized it admirably in a single sentence: "Truth for the mind, high emotion for the heart, heroic action for the will." Men need something to sweat and suffer for. They do not really live unless they have it. Christian evangelism is not a call to occupy the rocking chair of grace for the rest of one's natural—or unnatural—life. It is a challenge to take to the road in the discipleship of Him who will be forever on the road until the last man and the last area of human life are redeemed.

A friend of mine had a life-changing dream. Christ himself stood before her saying, "Come, go where I am going." "Where?" she asked. The answer: "You have done with places. Henceforth there is only one place—where I am." The vision fled. In deep fear of being left behind, she left the room crying, "Having seen what I have seen, I am going." She awoke trembling, but knew that she had discovered even in her sleep the only explanation she would ever give for her behavior: "Having seen what I have seen, I am going where I am going."

"If any man would come after me, let him deny himself and take up his cross daily and follow me." (Luke 9:23 R.S.V.) That is the summons of Christ. That should be our summons in his name. Evangelism is truly Christian only when it challenges the wills of men to follow him, to go where he is going, to seek no place except the place of his leading, and in that place to do his will as far as that is revealed to them.

# I SAW SATAN FALL

*Gerald Kennedy*

> The seventy returned with joy, saying, "Lord, even
> the demons are subject to us in your name!" And he
> said to them, "I saw Satan fall like lightning from
> heaven. Behold, I have given you authority to tread
> upon serpents and scorpions, and over all the power of
> the enemy; and nothing shall hurt you. Nevertheless
> do not rejoice in this, that the spirits are subject to
> you; but rejoice that your names are written in
> heaven."—Luke 10:17-20 (R.S.V.)

AN ENGLISH OFFICER ONCE MADE A HAZARDOUS JOURNEY INTO
Tibet on a vital mission for his government. He accomplished the
task with such calmness and assurance that someone asked him
the secret of his fearlessness. He replied: "It is twofold: (A) I have
been sent by unimpeachable authority for a purpose which is
sound. (B) If I get into a tight place, I have the government behind me, which would use all its resources to see me through." [1]

I read this and then began to think about the early Christians.
They went forth on a dangerous enterprise and yet they impressed their contemporaries with their courage and assurance.
Their simple fearlessness was nothing less than a miracle, and it
so impressed the Roman world that in spite of persecution and
death they conquered.

In the text we have a report of what might be called the first
visitation evangelism campaign ever conducted in the church.

---

[1] Leslie D. Weatherhead, *That Immortal Sea* (Nashville: Abingdon Press, 1953),
p. 65.

Whatever your criticism of this method of winning converts may be, do not try to suggest that it is new. Jesus had sent them out two by two, and they came back with shining eyes to report what had happened. Four things stood out in their testimony. First, they had an authority. "Behold, I have given you authority." Second, they had a purpose. They could set men free and change their lives. Third, they felt that the whole government of heaven was behind them. Fourth, they had a sense of victory. "I saw Satan fall." You could hardly find a better summary of the church's charter of evangelism.

## I

The early Christians had found that fundamental necessity of life, an authority to live by. Until this has been accomplished we build on the sand. A generation which makes a virtue out of a refusal to accept any ultimate value or recognize any absolute ends up finally by confessing that of such is the beginning of servitude.

Imagine a scene which might have taken place in an early Roman court. A group of Christians have been brought before the judge for examination and judgment. He is a decent, honest man, and he wants sincerely to know what this new religion is all about. "What is a Christian?" he asks.

One of the prisoners answers for them all. "A Christian, your honor, is one who follows Jesus Christ."

"So! and who was he?"

"Well, we believe he was the Messiah, the Son of God."

"Where is he now?" The judge knows the answer to this.

"He is dead—that is, he was killed."

"Oh? How did he die?"

"Well, actually he was executed, your honor. He was crucified."

"I see! He was a criminal, a traitor to the nation, a subversive."

"No, sir. His enemies used false testimony. His trial was a farce. Anyway, he did not stay dead. He rose from the grave. His friends and disciples saw him. He lives!"

At this the judge looks upon this nondescript group with some pity and much impatience. "Can you not see how foolish all of this is?" he asks. "Are you wiser than the leaders of the government? Is it reasonable that a messiah would end up like that?" And he thinks to himself that this Christianity will not be very difficult to exterminate for it is even more ridiculous than he had thought.

But he was wrong and Rome was wrong. Back of these simple people and their simple testimony was a conviction that God had spoken to them in Jesus, and their lives were under his will and command. Their way of life was not based merely on an opinion nor on a vague hypothesis. They were not unstable people under the temporary influence of a powerful emotion. These men and women and children were convinced that in Jesus they had found the highway of holiness and the truth of God. In a word, they had an authority and it made them invincible.

How different it is with us! If we are asked by what authority we live, we must answer that the question is not relevant because we have outgrown the idea of authority. Yesterday we followed that way, today we are on this path, and tomorrow it may be something quite different. At the end of the day I must look back over my life and confess that if there was any single principle guiding me, I cannot tell what it was. We move under pressure and we are pushed this direction or that according to what or who pushes the hardest. The most horrifying suggestion that can be made to us is that we should go alone or act contrary to the majority.

For most of us, the boss or our business is the authority by which we live. Our ethics are only what can be practiced without incurring a financial loss. For many, the unanswerable justification for any behavior is that to do differently would be to lose money. There is our authority! Not for us the nonsense of John Woolman who refused to make out a bill of sale for a slave when his employer demanded it. How many men have said in these days as a young man said to me, "I do not really approve of drinking, but I have to do it in my business." By what authority does such a one live?

And none of this is any good. It denies the dignity of a man's life. It sows fear in his soul. It gives us a sense of futility and dreariness. It promises success, but somehow the success is cheap and trivial. Mark this down! Until a man finds the spiritual authority for his life, his life is futile and empty.

One of the ancient records, which has always lifted up my heart and given me new courage every time I read it, comes down to us from ancient Smyrna. It dates the martyrdom of Polycarp, one of the great Christian leaders of the Second Century. "Statius Quadratus being Procounsul, but Jesus Christ being King forever." Majority opinion may be good enough for some decisions, but when it comes to the great choices of life, a man needs a king. To the early Christians, Jesus was the king, and in that experience they found the authority which made them unconquerable.

## II

In the second place, these early Christians discovered a worthy purpose. When they saw that what Christ had done for them, they could in his name do for others, it enlarged their lives. They were no longer merely fishermen, or tradesmen, or tax collectors, or farmers. They were evangelists entrusted with the good news of redemption and power. They returned with joy saying in effect: "This thing works. We can change lives. We can set men free."

A magazine cartoon some time ago showed a publisher ushering an author out of his office, and saying regretfully, "Your novel is excellent, but right now we're looking for trash." There is a parable for our day! There is a good life, we say, but just now we are exploring the possibilities of evil. There is nobility, but just now we are interested in being common. There is high endeavor, but just now we prefer the mediocre.

A few years ago, I read an interesting story in a San Francisco newspaper. It told about a prominent couple in the city who had given up their business and social life to seek religious experience. The husband went into a monastery and the wife went into a nunnery. It caused a great deal of comment that a Catholic couple should choose to give up everything they had attained and seek comfort and peace of mind by such an extreme method.

That story came back to me recently when a man and his wife, both doctors, told the members of the Board of Missions of The Methodist Church why they were volunteering as medical missionaries to Nepal. They were leaving a lucrative and successful practice and they were sacrificing relationships built up during more than twenty-five years in the same city. Why? To me, they seemed to be saying that to represent the Great Physician in a faraway place was the kind of purpose which would more than compensate for what they must leave behind. Let a man be directed to a large usefulness, and the external circumstances of his life assume a secondary importance.

Peter Cartwright, the famous Methodist circuit rider, relates in his *Autobiography* how he entered the ministry. He was converted when he was fifteen years old. He often testified of what the grace of Christ meant to him. In 1802, when he was seventeen, his family moved two or three counties west of Logan County, Kentucky. Peter wrote for a church letter and received instead a letter commissioning him to organize a new circuit in the wilderness. This was not quite what he had in mind and he objected. "I felt bad on the reception of this paper," he relates, "and told Brother Page I did not want to take it, for I saw through the solemn responsibilities it rolled upon me." [2] Yet this was the beginning of a great ministry and an exciting adventure. Our ways of earning our livings differ, but the main purpose of a Christian's life is ever the same. It is nothing less than being, in the name of Christ, a liberator of the people.

### III

Just as the young Englishman felt confident because his government had promised to stand back of him, so the Christians felt that all of God's government was back of them. Jesus' word to them was: "Nevertheless do not rejoice in this, that the spirits are subject to you; but rejoice that your names are written in heaven." To say it differently, the great thing is not immediate success, but the assurance that we are citizens of heaven and belong to the heavenly order. God with all his resources is back of us.

[2] *Autobiography of Peter Cartwright,* ed. Charles L. Wallis (Nashville: Abingdon Press, 1956) , p. 52.

It must be confessed that we do not always act like people aware of this backing. A young playwright persuaded a famous actor to preview his play. The actor dozed through it and when the lights went up, the author asked indignantly, "How could you sleep when you knew I asked you here for an opinion?" The actor replied quietly, "Young man, sleep *is* an opinion." In spite of our protestations the world is unimpressed by our dozing, our passiveness, our timidity, our compromise. Too often we seem to have forgotten that our names are written in heaven. We lack the alertness and confidence of men able to claim God's backing.

The early Christians exhibited such an unexpected strength that they constituted a wondrous surprise to their enemies. They were not at all impressive in terms of influence and power, and probably the Roman authorities foresaw no real difficulty in disposing of them. The odds were overwhelmingly against them when the contest was observed from any sensible point of view.

But the marvel was that the odds did not seem to make much difference. The unseen conviction that God was back of them could hardly be taken into account by the opposition, but it proved to be the hidden obstacle to all worldly enmity. Men cannot fight against God, nor can they fight successfully against men who feel that God is fighting with them. The man who assumes simply that big battalions are the decisive element fails to reckon with the big convictions.

This invisible power of God working through men stands as one of the inexplicable mysteries of human history. Sometimes men try to reduce it to just a matter of *morale,* but obviously it is much more. It is the feeling expressed by an ancient war poem in the Old Testament. After a victory against the Canaanites and the death of the enemy general, the prophetess Deborah sang of Israel's triumph which she was bold enough to suggest had universal implications. "From heaven fought the stars, from their courses they fought against Sisera" (Judg. 5:20 R.S.V.) was the way she phrased it.

God's divine order will not save us from defeats nor will it promise us an easy path. But to know that we have become a part of it through Christ removes every ultimate despair and every fear of permanent loss. With every passing year it gets greater and more magnificent. We are like Tintoretto, trying in vain to paint the sea, and then throwing his brushes aside and crying out: "It keeps growing greater! Nobody can paint it." Who can describe the majesty of the heavenly order of which we are members? The kings and empires of this world can never brighten citizens of such a kingdom.

# IV

One of the most amazing things on this earth is the faith that goodness must have the ultimate triumph. It simply will not be downed. It is summed up in Jesus' declaration that Satan cannot have the last word. "I saw Satan fall," said Jesus when the seventy returned and reported their victories. Was this a vision of the plain man's power to overcome all the forces of evil in the name of Jesus? I think it represents the Christian assurance that no matter what the odds may seem to be, if we belong to Christ, we are stronger than all the power of Satan.

Men who have the Christian heritage can never yield to what may seem like an inevitable defeat of righteousness. Victor Hugo describes the fall of Napoleon as not due to superior forces or tactics, but to the fact that "he embarrassed God." In the darkest day of the Battle of Britain, a people faced the dark future and the probable defeat by a cruel foe with a kind of mad, glorious confidence. I listened to the terrifying news of the Pearl Harbor debacle on December 7, 1941, but could not believe that the Axis tyranny could ever achieve a lasting victory.

This is a moral universe. Our confidence does not lie in our superior cleverness nor in our more abundant resources. We will never feel safe because we have more atomic weapons and bigger armed forces. We face tomorrow with courage and confidence because we believe in God. As we commit our ways unto him, we rest assured that we too shall see Satan fall like lightning.

Jesus Christ was a disappointment to many of his contemporaries as he is to many of ours. He did not fit the preconceived idea of what a messiah ought to be. They wanted a more spectacular figure with a more impressive display of power. We too find it difficult to be impressed with the quietness of love and the strength of good will. We turn to the loud and noisy idols. We worship at the shrines of gods who promise worldly triumphs. Our sin today, as always, is idolatry.

But the passing years proclaim that Christ's is the only lasting power and glory. He cannot be dismissed and forgotten, for even in the most discouraging circumstances, he reigns forever and forever. If he walks the weary roads of Palestine, still he reigns. They may spit on him and finally crucify him. Still he conquers. Jesus Christ is not only the source of our peace, but he is the source of our victory. Like those followers of old time, we know that the power of overcoming the evil is not in us, but in him.

A young officer had been given a difficult, important assignment and had failed miserably. To everyone's surprise, including the young man's, the colonel gave him another task of equal importance and danger. But this time he came through with such fine heroism that he was given a decoration. When the chaplain tried to congratulate him, the young officer cried out almost indignantly: "What else could I do? I failed the man and he went on trusting me." [3]

We do not always come through our testings as we wish we would. Yet time after time we are brought back to our tasks with renewed determination because of the trust our Lord puts in us. And always we seem to feel the assurance that through him the victory will be won. We have an authority; we have a purpose; we have the support of the divine government; we know the final victory is ours. For such men life becomes a great adventure and a glorious triumph.

[3] Adam W. Burnet in *The Sacramental Table*, ed. George Johnstone Jeffrey (New York: Harper & Bros., 1954), p. 45.

98

# AN ALTAR TO THE UNKOWN GOD

*John Sutherland Bonnell*

> As I passed by, and beheld your devotions, I found
> an altar with this inscription, TO THE UNKNOWN
> GOD. Whom therefore ye ignorantly worship, him
> declare I unto you.—Acts 17:23

JOHN KELMAN CALLS THE VISIT PAUL MADE TO ATHENS "ONE OF
the most picturesque and remarkable incidents recorded in the
whole history of religion." Only a writer of sound education and
culture, such as Luke the Greek physician, could have written a
document so replete with understanding and scholarship as the
seventeenth chapter of Acts.

John Milton describes Athens as the "eye of Greece, Mother
of Arts and Eloquence," and such it was when Paul visited this
famous city, though something of the glory had departed. On all
sides he beheld architectural magnificence, thanks to such states-
men as Themistocles, Cimon, and Pericles. Here too was located
the most famous university of the ancient world, in a real sense
the mother of all universities.

What notable men Athens had seen: Demosthenes, pouring
forth a torrent of eloquent words; Socrates, teaching his students
or offering his noble defense when on trial for his life; Phidias,
with his chisel and mallet bringing incomparable beauty out of
vast masses of marble; Hippocrates, the "father of medicine,"
pursuing his studies and writing his code of medical ethics which
is revered even to this day. And with these also were Zeno,
Epicurus, Plato, Aristotle, and other mighty thinkers who have

molded and influenced philosophic thought across more than two thousand years.

And now for the first time the apostle Paul looks upon this city of culture, of beauty, and of historic fame. Surely it was providential guidance that led Paul to Athens, for intellectually he stood head and shoulders above all the other apostles. So we find Peter the fisherman later writing that Paul, out of the wisdom God had granted him, had written epistles "in which are some things hard to be understood" (II Pet. 3:16). How true that was of Simon Peter's slower brain!

# I

An ancient proverb declared that "there are more gods in Athens than men." The apostle Paul found this to be true. Everywhere he looked—in niches, on pedestals, in temples, on street corners—everywhere were gods and demigods, a veritable wilderness of gods; and among them one significant altar "To the Unknown God." Righteous indignation swelled up in Paul's breast as he looked upon this idolatry. Had not the Eternal One declared: "Thou shalt have no other gods before me"? (Exod. 20: 3.)

But Paul was too wise a man to begin by attacking the religious institutions of these Athenians. Instead he went into the synagogues and preached; and in the agora, or public market, he mounted one of the rostrums provided and preached Christ to men and women of many races, to soldiers and sailors, to merchants and priests.

Now certain philosophers happened to drift by and listen to Paul. The concept of "resurrection" was new to them, so they thought that Paul was upholding two deities—"Jesus" and "Resurrection." These philosophers belonged to the Epicurean and Stoic schools. The Epicureans were pessimists who proclaimed that death ends all, and so they would be highly unfavorable to the idea of resurrection. The Stoics, on the other hand, believed in God as "the universal soul" of the world. These were the two chief schools of philosophy at Athens in Paul's time. At every point we are able to verify Luke's historical accuracy.

A.3278

These philosophers recognized in Paul a man of literary gifts and of no small dialectical ability, so they constrained the apostle to go with them to Areopagus. In the quiet surroundings of Mars' hill he could speak unhurriedly and answer their questions. They would give him a polite and not unfriendly hearing. This is thought by many authorities to be the very spot on which Socrates had defended his religious beliefs. Indeed Paul was in some respects a second Socrates because he too led men, as they sought after God, back from the contemplation of nature to the inner life of the spirit.

These Athenian lecturers and professors of the university whom Paul will now address are soon to discover that, despite their learning, he has much to teach them. We are not surprised to find that the apostle, who had said that he would become all things to all men in order to win them to Christ, now adapts his message to this unusual congregation.

There had been some resentment stirred up against Paul because he appeared to be offering foreign gods to the Athenians. They had a great sense of patriotic pride, and in the populace in general there was considerable religious fervor. Paul begins his address most diplomatically by declaring that he is not advocating strange gods. Indeed he wishes to commend to them a God whose altar stands at a crossroad in their own city—"The Unknown God." "I have come," said Paul, "to tell you of this Unknown God."

There is a most significant omission in this address by the apostle which differentiates it from all the rest of his discourses recorded in the New Testament: He makes no reference whatsoever to the Hebrew scriptures and does not appeal to these as his authority. The reason for this should be obvious. His usual approach would have had no meaning for the Athenians and he would have lost his audience at once. So instead of beginning with Abraham or with Jerusalem, he begins with Athens itself and the altar to "The Unknown God." "It is not then of a foreign god that I would speak," said Paul, "but the God to whom you have already erected an altar." The apostle was aware that every idol demonstrates the need for God, every temple the urge to

101

worship. Paul continues: "Now this God whom you have not known made the world and all things in it, and since he is Lord of heaven and earth he dwells not in temples made with hands nor does he need these manifold gifts you carry to many altars. This God is everywhere. Indeed he is close to all of us, for in him we live and move and have our being. Didn't one of your own poets, Aratus of Soli, who was also a physician, say in a prayer-poem: 'For we are indeed his offspring'?"

How skillfully Paul draws upon his knowledge of Greek literature! And now comes the master stroke of his argument. "Well, then, if we are God's offspring, why do you degrade him by representing him in gold or silver or stone, for then you are making this great God into a symbol that is far less than yourselves, who are his children? In doing this, you are denying the truth that your own poets have declared. You are lowering yourselves and dishonoring God."

"There was indeed a time," Paul added, "when God overlooked such things, for they were done in ignorance; but now a new hour has struck, a new day has dawned with the coming of his Son. Now God calls all men to repentance, for he will judge the world by this man, Jesus the Christ, who was crucified at Jerusalem but whom God has raised from the dead."

## II

Paul's address had a mixed reception—some were scornful, some were interested, and some were converted. Among them was one notable man, a philosopher and a member of this very court of Areopagus which Paul had been addressing.

For some time now it has been the custom among some Bible students to say that Paul's visit to Athens was a failure because so few converts are mentioned. But the few whose names are mentioned had only to do with one sermon, and it was preached to the sophisticated and cynical philosophers of Athens. There were undoubtedly other converts throughout the city where Paul had been preaching, and all of them were destined to form the nucleus of a Christian church.

It would appear that on this brief visit to Athens Paul accomplished all that could be expected. He established a Christian "beachhead," to borrow a word from military parlance, and that foothold was never lost. Why do we say this? Because of something that most sermons on the subject of Paul's visit to Athens and many of the commentaries have overlooked. In the very next century, perhaps only eighty years after Paul's visit, some of the ablest defenders of Christianity began to appear in this very city of Athens. I shall speak of only two in detail. Aristides was one of them. He was an Athenian philosopher of the second century and without a doubt a member of Areopagus. It was known for some centuries that he had written brilliantly in defense of Christianity, but the first full copy of his writings was discovered by Rendel Harris in the nineties of the last century at Mount Sinai monastery. It is a powerful argument in favor of the faith of Christ, and parts of it read like Paul's address on Mars' hill. Indeed that address may well have been used as a model by this philosopher.

A second great scholar, Athenagoras, was a native of Athens. He also wrote in the second century. Note this: he was a Platonic philosopher. And what was the theme of one of his greatest writings? Why, a defense of the Christian doctrine of the resurrection. Time would fail me to tell of other great Christian scholars, such as Publius and Quadratus, from second century Athens. Two centuries later came Basil the Great, who was trained in the University of Athens, and the renowned Gregory. All these notable men who did so much to sustain the faith of Christians in the early centuries of the church were but a part of the harvest of which Paul had planted the first seeds in his mission to Athens.

## III

What lessons for today does Paul's visit to Athens convey? First, the importance of a strong and intelligent presentation of the case for Christianity. The first three hundred years of the church's history was a time of utmost importance for our faith, and it was essential that the church should have able defenders to meet the attacks of the scholarly pagans of that era. That urgent need was met by men of such intellectual and spiritual caliber as Aristides and Athenagorus. Unfortunately there has been a tendency in some church circles in America to belittle the importance of a reasoned presentation of Christian truth. Our churches have a long tradition of belief, which must be maintained, in the necessity of an appeal to the mind as well as to the heart.

In the second place, pastors and teachers of the church should stand ever ready to adapt their presentation to the thought forms of the living present and to the level of the hearers' understanding. With these considerations in mind, special attention should be paid to the needs of tens of thousands of our American college people. What the educated believe today, the masses of the people will believe tomorrow. So too in our nation there are many men and women who are worshipers of "The Unknown God." To them we must declare the eternal gospel of the God and Father of Jesus Christ.

# 13

# GOD'S OUTREACH

*Ralph A. Herring*

Scripture: Luke 8:40-56

GOD REACHES IN TWO DIRECTIONS: HE REACHES DOWN AND HE reaches out. Most of us are better acquainted with his downreach than we are with his outreach. He reached down from heaven's heights to save us. Paul was thinking of this downreach when he wrote to his young friend Timothy, "Faithful is the saying, and worthy of all acceptation, that Christ Jesus came into the world to save sinners; of whom I am chief" (I Tim. 1:15 A.S.V.). The gulf God spanned is an up-and-down gulf, and each of us knows something about it. But God would reach out as well as down. It is at this point that those of us who have experienced the saving power of his downreach should be concerned. What of his outreach?

In vivid colors Luke the physician paints a life situation which in its essential respects is like that in which many worshipers find themselves today. A woman with a deep sense of need quietly joins the throng about Jesus. Her outstretched hand of faith taps God's healing power. "Immediately the issue of her blood stanched." (Luke 8:44 A.S.V.) Mark's account adds, "and she felt in her body that she was healed of her plague" (5:29 A.S.V.). Her purpose accomplished, she is about to go on her way, but the Great Physician would make far more of the incident.

The point of the story is not to be found in that which transpired between the woman and her Lord alone. Were that all, the errand to the home of Jairus would not have been interrupted.

105

The point is that this woman had felt the healing of God's down-reach and was about to go her way forgetful of his outreach. And Jesus would not let her do so. He had a lesson for her and for all of us who wish to remain unidentified partakers of his goodness, neglectful of the needs of others.

## I

What light, then, does this story shed upon God's outreach? It shows us how concerned the Lord Jesus is; for the extent of this concern can be gauged by the unusual things which it prompted him to do.

The situation in which Jesus found himself, from the human point of view, was one which required haste. A child hovering at the point of death, a famous Physician arriving at the city limits in the nick of time, a father whose urgent plea outweighs his prominence as a religious and social leader—these are factors which in our day would call for wailing sirens and a speeding ambulance. Jesus was in a hurry, that is, if he ever got in one! And yet all else must wait while he deliberately stops to deal with a woman who had no intention at all of interrupting his errand.

His concern for God's outreach upon this occasion, also, out-weighed his natural reluctance toward publicity. Upon first exami-nation this woman's quest for anonymity would seem to be in exact accord with his own way of doing things. Jesus often wrought his miracles in studied seclusion from curiosity seekers. On one occasion he had led a blind man outside the city to perform his cure, and on another he had sent ten lepers to show themselves to the priest rather than to effect healing in the presence of all. And shortly after healing the woman he was to exclude from the home of Jaïrus all but three of his disciples and the parents, when he called the child back to life and presented her to them.

We may be sure that it was not for his own sake that Jesus asked so insistently, "Who is it that touched me?" Nor was it for his own satisfaction that he turned the spotlight upon a timid woman, all but forcing her to make public the cherished secret of her healing. These unusual procedures emphasize his concern for others besides the woman herself. The flow of God's power had healed her, but he longed to reach out through her to others. He simply could not let his healing energy be grounded in the woman herself. Others were involved—Jairus, and for that matter, all the rest of us.

The Savior knew that the ruler of the synagogue was about to hear the saddest words ever to fall on a father's ear. He knew also that this heartbroken man was about to enter his supreme hour. The faith that prompted him to leave his daughter's bedside in quest of Jesus must be strong to meet the coming test. Everything depended upon the quality of that faith. Only thus could the way be open for the Lord of Life to restore his daughter. He could not let this woman stop in her isolation. Her testimony must nourish the faith of Jairus. He had reached down to her; he must reach out through her, for such is ever his way.

For seven years it was my privilege to serve as pastor in Ashland, Kentucky. In the mountains of that region coal mines are a familiar sight, their shafts sunk deep into the heart of the earth. I can imagine that the sinking of those shafts was done at great expense and that the cost involved was never justified by the amount of coal found at the bottom of the shaft. Returns upon the investment were always through the outreach from the shaft as miners followed the rich vein of coal.

In this matter of salvation, as with mining, it is the outreach that pays for the operation. The downreach is necessary. God has paid a fearful price to provide it. The importance of this vertical relationship between man and his God cannot be overemphasized. All supplies and equipment come by this route. The reward, however, will be found upon our own level—the pay-off comes in the outreach.

Certainly there can be no vital worship except as we get in touch with God, but such an experience cannot be satisfying from his point of view nor complete in its highest meaning for ourselves apart from an outreach which brings him into living touch with others. All that Jesus does for us reflects only a small part of his concern in comparison with that which he desires to do through us.

## II

This interesting passage of scripture, however, reveals not only our Lord's great concern for God's outreach, but also the chief point at which that outreach is so often blocked. Here was a woman who desired to conclude her experience with Jesus with her own healing. Although she could not at that time fully realize the consequences, she was content to let the faith of Jairus sicken and die for want of encouragement and to strike out of the pages of the New Testament one of its most remarkable testimonies to the grace of God. Is she so different from us in this respect?

In seeking an answer to this question, I remind you of the nature of her affliction and the distressing condition to which it had brought her. The record indicates that she had suffered from her malady for a period of twelve years. According to the Jewish ceremonial law she was regarded as unclean. It would be surprising indeed if such a case history had not wrought with devastating effect upon her emotions. According to tradition she had once been a woman of means and high social standing, but her quest for health had reduced her to poverty. We can well understand, therefore, how a justifiable pride, a sense of modesty, would prompt her to shun public attention.

But let us examine a little more closely this state of mind which we are about to excuse with such sympathetic understanding. Because the colors of the rainbow run the gamut of the spectrum from violet to red, a ray of white light can never be understood apart from the more somber hues of its lower frequency. In somewhat the same manner, motives which appear to us innocently white must be made to pass through the spectrum of reality before their baser elements can be observed.

We begin with that in the woman's attitude which can cause no offense—her modesty. But the shade deepens quickly—modesty, timidity, reserve, embarrassment, pride, selfishness, sin. A timidity or reserve, call it what you may, that would shut off the flow of saving power, forgetful of the glory of God and the needs of others, is sin. It is the kind of sin that does the most damage because it appears to us so appropriate to our circumstances. It is pride in reverse, evading reality, by slipping out the backdoor of humility. Such pride can be found in many places hiding behind reserve and a false sense of propriety.

I think I see a touch of this sort of thing in Martha's remonstrance to Jesus as they stood together at the gravestone of her brother Lazarus. "Take ye away the stone" (John 11:39 A.S.V.), Jesus had said. Martha was instantly horrified by the embarrassing prospect. Laying a restraining hand upon his arm, she said, "Lord, by this time the body decayeth." We can understand how she felt. Jesus was about to offend the propriety of the occasion and she would stop him. Had he yielded to her insistence there would have been no raising of Lazarus from the dead. Pride, that most subtle of all sins, was on the point of robbing the crown jewel from the diadem of miracles which John was to place upon the head of him who is the Resurrection and the Life.

Very often that which keeps the lid on a malodorous situation also keeps out the sweet breath of cleansing and life. To shut some things in can mean to shut Jesus out. We must judge sin not by its appearance but by its effect. God sees it as a defalcation, a shortage. "For all have sinned, and *fall short of the glory of God.*" (Rom. 3:23 A.S.V.) We must recognize that the sin of omission deprives an occasion of its highest meaning far more often than the transgression of certain laws of propriety, whether human or divine.

We who love our Bibles would become instantly indignant at anyone who would tear from its pages the beautiful story of the way Lazarus was restored to the Bethany home, or of the way in which healing virtue flowed upon the touch of faith into the weakened body of a woman who for so long a time had been troubled by an incurable malady. But we are often guilty of the same vandalism under the innocent guise of natural timidity or reserve. Through fear of embarrassment we have also robbed many an occasion of its eternal glory. The desire to hide one's identity in the throng that follows Jesus, to remain the anonymous recipients of God's grace, is widespread and damaging. It is a subtle expression of self-interest, and I am persuaded that it constitutes the chief point of stoppage in God's outreach to others.

### III

In the passage before us Jesus deals with this situation in a masterful fashion. Step by step he builds up the pressure to the point where the woman comes out in the open with the whole story. The account of her experience reaches down through the ages to inspire our faith. Her fear and trembling serve only to strengthen her testimony.

The implications of this story are heart-searching because God reaches out today as he did then. The record reads, "She came trembling, and falling down before him declared in the presence of all the people for what cause she touched him, and how she was healed immediately." (Luke 8:47 A.S.V.) Why? and How? are searching questions to answer before God and in the presence of our fellow men. They roll up the blinds to the windows of our souls and allow others to see what God has wrought within.

There is one word to describe Christ's remedy for this obstruction to his outreach, but I hesitate to use it because it has come to have a restricted, almost technical connotation; yet, I hardly see how we can do without it from this point onward in our discussion. It is the word "confession." Too often confession has been limited to matters involving guilt. In the New Testament however the word has a far wider application than that, as we shall see. But before exploring these wider applications, we shall do well to consider for a moment how effectively God reaches out to others when we honestly and humbly confess our sins.

Sin with its burden of guilt is the one thing which the human race has in common. It is the most persistent problem in any life. When someone finds the answer and is delivered from that burden, others are immediately interested in the story. A world which turns a deaf ear to the preachment of saints will thus respond with warm interest to the testimony of sinners saved by grace. Yes, God reaches out through the confession of sins.

In our church some years ago a worshiper made his way forward one morning during the singing of the invitation hymn.

His face was bathed with tears, and as he spoke a few broken words in my ear he pressed into my hands an item which he had torn from the morning's newspaper. Hurriedly I glanced at the headlines. It was a report of his arrest in connection with some shameful conduct in which he had been involved the week before. He had come forward to ask the forgiveness of the church against which he had sinned. "I feel that God has forgiven me," he said, "but I want the people to know how ashamed I am and to forgive me also." That forgiveness was quickly granted, but the thing that impressed me was the way in which the congregation responded. Tears came to many eyes. People who had sat unmoved through the service felt suddenly and afresh the power of the gospel. I have long since forgotten the subject of my sermon that morning, as I am sure the congregation has, but I shall never forget the incident in which a penitent sinner bared his heart to let us see God's grace at work.

The idea involved in testimony is very close kin to that which we have been discussing. Confession in its wider sense includes testimony. When representatives of the Sanhedrin in Jerusalem interviewed John the Baptist, "He confessed, and denied not; and he confessed, I am not the Christ" (John 1:20 A.S.V.). This confession was simply John's testimony. It was his way of keeping the record straight, his response to the truth.

## IV

Much is being said today about mass evangelism and personal evangelism. Many good and helpful approaches have been discovered and put into effect, and we are grateful for them all. We are rightly concerned about methods and all the outreaching agencies of the church, but there is something with which we must come to grips on a level deeper than that of methods. There must be a certain transparency of life whereby that which God works within may shine forth to others about us.

It is easier to open the windows of the soul to God than to our fellow men. Hypersensitiveness toward the opinion of others and bondage to a misguided conception of the propriety of an occasion are factors which draw down the shades. Effectively, though unintentionally, we thus keep the light from others. But humility throws open the blinds. Forthrightness and unstudied simplicity are qualities of the soul which know they have nothing to lose but everything to gain by coming out into the light before God and men. I like to think of humility in terms of transparency, as the clear waters of a mountain spring without sediment of self, or as the windowpane which serves best when unobserved. May God give us such transparency of life that others may see the glory of his amazing grace reaching down through Jesus Christ to work within our own experience.

It would hardly be fair, I think, to take our leave from this passage without realizing that the downreach and outreach are in God's sight one and the same thing. His downward reach is never what he would have it until it extends outward. And each outward impulse is but the projection and the perfection of that which was given from above. Of all who were benefited by the woman's full confession, no one profited more than the woman herself. The experience meant a cleansing of her own faith. The fires of embarrassment from which she shrank purged away the superstition of her own preconceived notions. She learned that salvation flows not through physical contact but through faith, and she heard the benediction of Jesus, "Go in peace." God's downreach and God's outreach work together in perfect harmony. Actually they complete a gracious cycle, the one extending the other only to find itself strengthened and enriched.

# 14

# OUT WHERE THE NEW BEGINS

*Paul S. Rees*

> So if anyone is in union with Christ, he is a new
> being; the old state of things has passed away; there
> is a new state of things.—II Cor. 5:17 (Goodspeed)

A FULL PAGE NEWSPAPER ADVERTISEMENT BY A NATIONAL BUSINESS
magazine had this lead-line: "Out where the new begins." Beneath was the story of a successful merchandiser of heavy machinery who joined a new company to sell a new metal fabricating machine, and in so doing introduced a new approach to the problem of successful marketing.

The story is incidental, but the headline appealed to me because I knew, as every spiritually transformed Christian knows, that out where the new really begins is not Pittsburgh, Detroit, Lima, or Moline, but where a man meets Jesus Christ. Into this realm of radical spiritual newness each of us has been or can be brought. Our Lord expressed this imperatively when he said, "Ye must be born again" (John 3:17). In our text Paul says conditionally, "If anyone is in union with Christ, he is a new being; the old state of things has passed away; there is a new state of things."

Does the phrase "in Christ" or "in union with Christ" puzzle you? To many people the words are meaningless, which of course indicates that the new life has never invaded them. Yet these people apparently know what you mean when you say that you are in politics, in law, in business, or in advertising.

If a man says that he is in politics, for example, you know that politics has become the ruling interest, the controlling passion of

113

his life. You know that in his absorption in politics may be found a decision and a commitment. The decision was to make politics his career to the exclusion of other careers, and this decision was followed by his commitment of himself—his time and energies and training—to this chosen field of action.

In principle it is not otherwise with conversion and the spiritually changed life. The person who is "in Christ" is the person who has decided for Christ. For him there are not a dozen saviors, but one—Jesus Christ, crucified and risen. Nor is that all. He has completely committed himself to Christ. "The only faith which makes a Christ," said Martin Luther vigorously, "is that which casts itself on God for life or death." Such a decision and such a commitment opens the floodgates of the life which flows from Christ, and a new creation is begun.

Of what does this newness consist? Paul's answers deserve our consideration.

I

First is *a new relationship to God:* "all things are of God, who hath reconciled us to himself by Jesus Christ" (II Cor. 5:18). The Bible is blunt and stubborn in its insistence that mankind is in rebellion against God. This rebellion, curiously enough, is not primarily against the idea of God or against a sentimental recognition of God; it is fundamentally against the reign of God, the control of God, the will of God.

This rebellion is the fruitful source of all sorts of evil, conflict, strife, anxiety, and frustration. Man, having moved over from his true center in God to a false center in himself, finds that nothing comes out right. He is an alien in a world where he should feel at home. He is a warrior in a world where he should be a peacemaker. He is a slave in a world where he should be free. He is a fool in a world where he should be wise. He is a destroyer in a world where he should be a builder. He is time's vagabond in a universe where he should be eternity's pilgrim.

The glory of the gospel is that in such a confused world as this a Cross has been erected. And at that Cross the most wonderful thing in all the range of human experience takes place. There, where Jesus Christ's atoning death writes the message of God's forgiving, healing love in letters of holy blood, the rebel becomes a citizen, the alien is at home, the slave is made free, the fool sees the light, and earth's wanderer sets out for the celestial city. In the center of this whole experience of change is a new relationship to God—reconciliation—which has come through our acceptance of his Son as our Mediator and Savior.

If you ask how and when that acceptance takes place, the only honest answer is that no two cases are exactly alike. I think of two quite opposite instances of conversion: one that of an influential layman, the other of a university girl.

The layman was a friend and helper of Dwight L. Moody. His name was Daniel W. McWilliams and he was an elder in the Presbyterian Church. Not only did he constantly work to win men to Christ, but he also gave generously to open the Presbyterian mission in Korea. Yet this man, who saw scores of other men spiritually reborn, had no recollection of his own conversion. That he had been converted he did not doubt. Some would say that because he had Christian parents and grew up in a Christian home he needed no conversion. But that was never his explanation. He said that his acceptance of Jesus Christ as his Savior occurred so early in childhood that the precise moment had failed to carry over into adult memory. Although he did not have a recollection that went back to the event of conversion, he did have an assurance of faith that proclaimed the fact of conversion. So instead of growing up as a wanderer from Christ, he grew up as a follower of Christ. Instead of becoming a hardened rebel against God, he early gave his will and trust to God and, through Christ, was reconciled to God.

The college girl came to me one night after I had spoken at her school. She said that something in my message had prompted her to relate a chapter from her spiritual experience. The recital that followed was in some respects shocking. There was, for example, a period in her middle teens when she had been so self-willed and defiant toward God that more than once, while listening to a minister's appeal for lives to be surrendered to Christ, she prayed to the devil for strength to resist Christ's call.

115

Her soul was a battleground on which she fought God as if he were her worst enemy. But the day came when the Love that would not let her go broke through her resistance, captured her heart, and transformed her life. Through surrender to Christ, the God-center that every life needs became hers and a new dawn spread across her sky.

"Out where the new begins" is where we find, through the crucified Jesus, a new relationship to God. We stand no longer condemned, but forgiven; no longer prodigals, but sons in the Father's house.

## II

Consider, in addition, that to be born anew in Christ means *a new regard for others:* "henceforth know we no man after the flesh" (II Cor. 5:16). To comprehend the meaning of this statement let us turn to other translations. Goodspeed renders these words: "I have estimated nobody at what he seemed to be outwardly." The Revised Standard Version reads: "We regard no one from a human point of view." And Arthur Way translates: "So from henceforth we appraise no man by human standards."

If you look at human beings through the eyes of sinful, selfish, prejudiced, bigoted men, you get one view. If you look at human beings through the eyes of Jesus Christ, you get a very different view. Paul is saying that when you base your concern for people on their wealth or their poverty, you are not judging them with a Christian appraisal. If you base your concern on their being of a certain color, whether black or white or otherwise, you are not judging them according to the mind of Christ.

From the Christian point of view the most significant thing about people is that they are people—not that they are clever or stupid, not that they are Caucasian or Negro, not that they are "on relief" or in the social register, but that they are the creatures of the Lord God Almighty. Furthermore, they are people for whom Jesus Christ died! That gives them, one and all, a claim to distinction that all the foolish egotisms and prejudices of men can never remove.

Appraising man by man's manufactured standards is dangerous.

It is a flowing spring whence come many poisoned streams. A neighbor saw a pastor's boy playing with a Jewish lad, and proceeded to say to him, "As a good Christian you must hate the Jews." The little fellow looked at that frightfully warped adult and replied: "Jesus was a Jew, wasn't he?" I can confidently say that this person was not a typical or representative Christian. It is clear, you see, that our youngsters get their prejudices from the oldsters, not from any natural hostilities.

A white boy declared, "I was sixteen years old before I knowed I was any better'n a Negro." He had to be drilled into looking upon Negro children according to man's standards instead of Christ's standards.

"Out where the new begins" is where a new relation to God is established and a new regard for others is created. Have you been there?

## III

Paul tells us that those who belong to Christ's new creation have *a new reason for living:* "for the love of Christ constraineth us" (II Cor. 5:14). "The very spring of our actions is the love of Christ" is Phillips' paraphrase of these words.

Almost anyone can tell you his reason for making a livelihood, but few can tell you their reason for living. We make a livelihood in order to have food on our tables and clothes on our backs. But that doesn't make a life.

A pastor, talking with a group of college students in their fraternity house, turned to the chairman of the meeting and asked, "What are you living for?" The student answered, "I am going to be a pharmacist." The pastor said, "I understand that this is how you are going to earn your livelihood, but what are you living for?" The youth thought for a moment and then in a manner that suggested both honesty and bewilderment said, "Sir, I am sorry, but I haven't thought that through." And when asked the same question, only two of the thirty young men had seriously faced the central issue of existence, our reason for living.

The Christian has an answer to that basic question, and the greatest Christian of the centuries has expressed it in these priceless words: "The love of Christ constraineth us." To be the channel through which the love of Christ flows is the reason for living. Can you name a higher or more compelling one?

In the fifteenth verse the apostle enlarges upon this master motive in Christian living: Christ "died for all, that they which live should not henceforth live unto themselves, but unto him which died for them, and rose again."

Yield yourself to the love of Christ, and you will be swept out of the love of self. And his love will do more, for it will not only sweep you *out* but sweep you *on*. By an inner and insistent compulsion it will give drive and direction to your personality and all its dedicated powers.

One night when Dwight L. Moody was preaching in a great hall in London, a young medical student, who had quite casually said, "I am going to see what a Yankee evangelist looks like," was in the crowd. Moody began preaching. His eyes were bright and searching, his words falling like a power-driven hammer. Before long he said vigorously: "Let God have your life. He can do more with it than you can. Let God have your life!" How little did the evangelist realize that his words were ordained by the spirit of God to stab that young student out of his easygoing self-interest and fling open before him a whole new world of living. He became a new man, a man who had taken Jesus Christ as his Savior, a man whose whole reason for living had been suddenly changed. Who was the man? Sir Wilfred Grenfell, missionary-doctor to the neglected people of Labrador, who through all the years that followed could say with Paul: "The love of Christ constraineth us."

"Out where the new begins!" That is where you find, in Christ, a new relation to God, a new regard for others, a new reason for living—and one thing more.

## IV

You also find a new restfulness concerning the life that lies beyond: "For we know that if our earthly house of this tabernacle were dissolved, we have a building of God, an house not made with hands" (II Cor. 5:1). Strictly speaking, this is Paul's way of proclaiming the doctrine of the resurrection and the glorified body which the Christian will one day receive. For our present purpose, however, it stands as a bracing testimony to the total fact of the future life, of survival beyond death, resurrection at Christ's second coming, and everlasting blessedness in heaven.

The Christian, the man who has been spiritually reborn by being united to Christ through faith, does not try to *prove* immortality. He *experiences* it. He knows that what he has in Christ, this life that possesses and controls him, has the "feel" of eternity. He knows what John meant when he declared:

Behold, what manner of love the Father hath bestowed upon us, that we should be called the sons of God. . . . Beloved, now are we the sons of God, and it doth not yet appear what we shall be: but we know that, when he shall appear, we shall be like him; for we shall see him as he is. (I John 3:1-2.)

A new relationship to God, a new regard for others, a new reason for living, a new restfulness about the life beyond—these are some of the revolutionary novelties, as enduring as they are excellent, that one finds "out where the new begins." Have you found it so? If not, there is a new life waiting for you now. It is not in a sermon, nor in a church, nor in a book. It is in Christ. Take him. Open your being to him. Confess your deadness to him. Trust him. "He that believeth on the Son hath everlasting life." (John 3:36.)

# 15

# CAN YOU RECOMMEND YOUR RELIGION?

*John A. Redhead*

He first findeth his own brother Simon, and saith
unto him, We have found the Messiah.—John 1:41

STUDENTS OF THE AMERICAN ECCLESIASTICAL SCENE ARE BECOMING
aware of a new movement which seems to be springing up. It is
called personal evangelism, as opposed to mass evangelism. It has
a motto according to which "each one will reach one." The genius
of the movement is that the individual church member, the layman, as over against the professional preacher, is the evangelizing
agent.

When a preacher stands in the pulpit and says that it is the duty
of the Christian to give himself to this business, you then have a
right to ask what is meant by evangelism. The best definition I
know comes from the late William Temple: "Evangelism is the
winning of men to acknowledge Christ as their Saviour and King,
so that they give themselves to this service in the fellowship of
the Church." According to that definition, the professional is not
the only evangelist. Any man who can recommend his religion
so as to lead another to take Christ as his Savior and King and to
give himself to the service of Christ in the fellowship of the
church is doing the work of the evangelist.

I

That this kind of thing is a part of the business of being a
Christian is entirely in line with biblical example. The Great
Commission was not given to the Christian ministry but to the

Christian church. It seems quite clear that when Jesus met his disciples on the mountain in Galilee about five hundred brethren were together in obedience to his summons. It was to this group, probably containing all who stood the shock of the crucifixion and maintained the integrity of the faith beyond it, that he gave the commission.

Furthermore, Paul says that pastors, teachers, and evangelists were given to the church for "the perfecting of the saints for the doing of service." The King James version, "for the perfecting of the saints, for the work of the ministry" (Eph. 4:12), gives the impression that the perfecting of the saints and the work of the ministry are two separate phases of the work of pastors. But other translations correct the error. They say that these gifts were given "for the perfecting of God's people *for* their appointed service," in order fully to equip them for the work of building up of the body for Christ, which is the growth of the church.

In other words, the task of recruiting for the church is placed not solely on the shoulders of the preacher but is to be shared by the layman. The pastor is not a religious lecturer but a spiritual general who marshals the forces under his charge and trains them for their appointed service, for the recruiting of others for the building up of the body of Christ.

Such a theory finds illustration in the gospel narrative. Here is a layman named Andrew. He is just a plain man who one day saw Jesus and was so impressed with him that he went home with him for further knowledge. Having convinced himself, we are told in the text that he first findeth his own brother Simon and saith unto him, "We have found the . . . Christ. . . . And he brought him to Jesus" (John 1:41-42). It is as simple as that. Each one reaching one. A man recommending his religion so that another is laid hold on by it.

It is interesting to me to note how we act upon this principle in other spheres and ignore it altogether in the church. During the summer before I went to college for the freshman year, I received two letters from men who lived in different states and of whom I had never heard before. Each said he had been informed I had registered for entrance in the college where he was a student and wanted to welcome me to the campus. It made me happy to know that I was going to a school where students were so thoughtful and friendly. But on arrival I found that these two men belonged to the same fraternity and that their letters were written not so much in behalf of the school as of the fraternity. They met the train, introduced me to others of the brethren, helped me to get matriculated and find a room, were most attentive in their rushing, and one day came as a group to invite me to join them. Fraternities do not leave the matter of recruiting to some paid leader whose business it is to replenish the ranks. Each one is on the lookout to find another who will make a good brother. They even write letters to those whom they have never met. I wonder how many members of the fraternity of Christ have ever written a letter or otherwise rushed a prospect to get him to join. But if for Kappa this and Kappa that, why not for Christ?

Another day a man who is an officer in the Presbyterian Church called and made a date. He had something he wanted to talk about, he said. When he came he brought a second man with him. He had come, he said, to talk about joining a civic club. He enjoyed his membership and he thought I would do the same, and he had gone to the trouble of having my name approved by the membership committee. I wonder how many officers in the Presbyterian Church had ever called and made a date with a man and gone to talk with him about joining a fellowship which is more than a civic club. But if for Kiwanis, why not for Christ?

## II

The principle of the layman as evangelist is not only right, it is reasonable. It is reasonable because the layman has so many favorable opportunities to introduce a man to Christ. Himself legion, he can get closer to so many more types of people, is acquainted with their peculiar needs, can speak their language, and is freer from the suspicion of professionalism. Let a minister talk to a man about religion and he will shrug his shoulders and say to himself, "That's his business," and think no more of it. But let a layman whose judgment he trusts and whose character he admires speak a good word for Christ, and it goes farther.

The parent, having an inside track with his sons and daughters to which no minister has a right to aspire, should count it his deepest duty and highest privilege to see to it that no son or daughter will ever grow up in his home and go out to face the world without spiritual resources which enable him to stand against it. The Sunday-school teacher, having an insight into the minds of the members of his class which the minister can never achieve, is able to strike when the iron is hot, as did that Sunday-school teacher who walked into a shoe store in Boston and persuaded a young salesman named Dwight L. Moody to sign on the dotted line. The businessman knows his employees and knows when an invitation is most likely to be accepted. The lawyer meets his clients on their own grounds and understands their points of view. The insurance man who talks security in the realm of the material can easily shift over to security in the spiritual. I know a real estate man who, as soon as he has found a house for a client, says, "Now that you have a home for your family, what about a church home for your spirit?" Of all the professions, the doctor has the chance par excellence. The very effectiveness of his skill in practising demands that his patients love him, trust him, follow his directions; and if he carries his religion as a stock in trade and recommends it as good medicine, his advantage as an evangelist is beyond all compare.

We all have friends. I was calling on a family in another city who were members of our church, and noticed on the table a beautifully engraved card which carried an invitation to a public meeting of another religious group. At the bottom of the card, written in ink, were the words, "Mary and John." The lady of the house said, "Yes, these are friends of ours and they have often talked to us about their religion and suggested that we try it." Strangely enough, I was not angry at such rank proselyting of good Presbyterians; I was only envious because we did not have in our church more men and women who were willing to use the privilege of friendship as a means of introducing their friends to a higher friendship.

To expect one minister to preach the gospel effectively to forty different types of people, each with his own viewpoint and vernacular, is as ridiculous as to expect him to be able to preach effectively in forty different langauages. The business of the layman as evangelist is not only right, it is reasonable too.

## III

There is one more thing to say. Personal evangelism is not only right and reasonable, it is also rewarding.

A man is rewarded by a deeper experience of his own faith. Your only requirement is that you have something to recommend. When we find something we like in other fields, we don't hesitate to recommend it: a new brand of pipe tobacco, a new wrinkle in a golf swing, a new lure for fishing, a new method of making rolls. Does your religion have anything in it that you can recommend? If not, then you are being cheated. And if the business of recommending it to someone else can make you put your finger on what it means to you, then it has done you a favor. The more often you recommend it, the more worth recommending it will become. We are so made that no mental or spiritual possession is really ours until we have expressed it, and the fuller and more frequent the expression, the more complete the possession. The reason insurance men regard so highly the policies they have to sell is that they have told so many people about them. Sit down and tell a man what your religion means to you and it will mean more.

Furthermore, when a layman sees himself as a minister of God engaged in the business of recommending his religion, he will have a high opinion of himself which will save him from many a pitfall in conduct. The layman expects his preacher to be above reproach in his living, and he has a right to do so. His very expectation helps to keep his preacher there. It keeps him from going certain places, doing certain things, telling certain stories, and following certain people. The vocation of the ministry is a strong moral safeguard. When the layman sees that as a Christian he is also a minister of God whose business it is to win men to Christ, and when he realizes that what he is talks so loud folks can't hear what he says, he will find the same uplifting power of a higher vocation.

When he helps to further the process of conversion in a life—

the process by which a person hitherto divided, unhappy, inferior, and consciously wrong becomes, under the touch of Christ, united, adequate, happy, and consciously right—he will have the pleasure of knowing he has done the man, and possibly the man's family, the greatest favor that can be done. Some of us feel that in Christ we have the final answer to the meaning of life. Far and away the deepest satisfaction any minister knows is to help a man find his way into the kingdom of God and, upon entering, to get his hands on the pearl of great price.

Finally, he is rewarded by the knowledge that he has done the heart of God good. One sentence in the report of a committee on evangelism at Presbytery so impressed one man I know that he reported it to the officers upon his return. The chairman had said this: "There is more joy in heaven over one sinner that repenteth than over ninety-nine church members at a fellowship dinner." We major in fellowship in our churches, and that is important; but when a man helps another find God he has the pleasure of knowing not only that he has helped himself and the man, but has brought joy in heaven.

I have on my shelf a little volume of sketches of Scottish peasant life entitled *Beside the Bonnie Brier Bush.* Perhaps you will remember the chapter entitled "His Mother's Sermon." It tells of how the young minister, John Carmichael, fresh from the theological seminary, a bit green and somewhat well satisfied with himself but with a heart at bottom sound and true, returned home to his remote rural parish. He supposed that a man who had taken the McWhammel prize in the seminary should on his first appearance in his remote parish give the people some instruction as to the present drift of liberal theological thought. He accurately prepared an elaborate essay with learned references to "Semitic environment" and the like. His godly maiden aunt was troubled when she discovered what kind of fare he was preparing to give the people on his first Sunday. With an instinctive tact she managed to remind him of a scene some years before, when he had kneeled at the bedside of his mother; she had reached out a trembling and emaciated hand and laid it on his head and expressed the hope that he would someday become a minister, and told him that if he did she would be there on the day he preached his first sermon. "And, oh, laddie," she said, "speak a gude word for Jesus Christ."

When the young man was reminded of that scene his face went white, and he arose and went to his study and took the elaborate discourse on which he had expended so much toil and put it into the glowing grate and saw it disappear in flame and smoke; and then set himself to prepare his mind and heart to speak a "gude word for Jesus Christ." On Sunday morning when he rose in the pulpit he was so much agitated that he omitted two petitions from the Lord's Prayer, but when he began to deliver his message the people had lost sight of the man before them and saw only the holy face of the Man of Nazareth. As the preacher proceeded, the rugged faces of those Scottish peasant men were softened as when the evening light falls on the granite cliff. When the service was over, someone asked old Donald Menzies what he thought of the new preacher and he would only answer, "There was a man sent from God and his name was John."

To speak a "gude" word about Jesus Christ is your business and mine.

# IV

## Brotherhood

# 16

# ON GETTING ALONG WITH EACH OTHER

*Samuel M. Shoemaker*

IT IS NOT TOO MUCH TO SAY THAT, SECOND ONLY TO FAITH IN GOD, our human relationships are the most important thing in our lives. We are generally happy when we are getting along reasonably well with other people, and we are generally unhappy when we are not. Few people are ever "successful" as the world sees success unless they know how to get along with other people; and many fail, in the worldly sense and in the Christian sense also, because they do not.

## I

The chief reason why many of us fail in this second most important thing in the world is that we have a false idea of how to create good human relationships. There are several groups of people who fall into this category.

There are the *dominators*. These are the people who move into a human situation and "take over." They talk more than other people; they try to get the attention of the group. In business they may be suave outwardly, but all the while they are scheming to get ahead of somebody else. At home they make everybody kowtow to them, and all plans begin with what pleases them. They may do this by the assertion of the man's right to be the head of the household, or by a ready bad temper which nobody in the family wants to arouse if it can be avoided. Or they may do it by whining and tears, the poor little woman being the family drudge and a martyr to everybody else. Some of the most dominating people in the world are outwardly the most simpering-sweet. Let's face it. There is as much of the dominator in most of us as we can get away with, unless we have given God some chance to control us.

Correlative with the dominators are the *doormats*. These are the people who find it easier to get along if they give in. If you live in the house with a steam roller, the nearer you come to the shape of a doormat, the less you get mashed in the process. I knew a man of considerable parts who early in life married an extremely dominating woman. He had had a dominating father as well, and between the two of them he hardly called his soul his own. His wife needed whatever corresponds in civilized society to a horsewhip. But this man thought discretion better than valor, and no one ever stood up to her self-will nor to his willingness to become a doormat. Underneath their acquiescence the doormats seethe with resentment and frustration, for their situation is an epitome of injustice. But some never muster the courage to break out of the old round of merely "giving in" as the best solution they know.

A third group are the *double talkers*. These people say one thing to one person or group, another to another person or group. They have never learned that, while this salves and smooths the situation for the moment, it makes for much more trouble in the end. To a person who has taken a strong line with another they say, "I think you acted perfectly right"; but to the second person they say, "Wasn't that a cruel and unnecessary thing that he did to you?" Somewhere there is truth and justice in the situation, but it takes time and patience and considerable courage to look for it and stand by it. The smartest thing seems to be to trim their sails and say what they think the people concerned want them to say—and thus let the whole situation down.

Let me give an illustration of what I mean. Here is a man who gets along poorly with his wife. He thinks it is all the wife's fault and says so. She thinks it is mostly his fault and says so. A relative who knows them both well enters the situation and deals with each one about *his* and *her* sins—*not* the other party's. Some frank, honest words are said which produce a beginning of real conviction of sin in this man. But he calls in a third party as counselor and tells him what has happened. The third party knows as well as everybody else that what has been said by the relative is the truth, but he has reasons for wishing to stand well with this man. So he takes color from the man with the stung conscience, says the relative was too severe in what he said, lets down the work of conviction the Holy Spirit of truth has begun, and fouls up the whole situation worse than it was. Meantime the third party himself comes off very successfully, as he thinks, standing well with everybody, facing nobody's resistance, but not daring to deal lovingly with the truth which alone could have made the situation right. This is not diplomacy; this is cowardice. I know men and women who will say one thing to one person, and turn right around and say the very opposite to another. Sometimes these people think themselves tactful for being able to see both sides, but actually they are without the courage to deal in the truth. The double talkers are always hopeless to help in a human situation that needs help. They do more harm than any other group, in the family, in the business, and in the church—in fact, wherever they are.

If you have a genuine criticism or objection, go to the person immediately involved and, with as much grace and good will as you can muster, take it up with him. What we usually do is to go to someone else, spill our "gripes" and criticisms, enlist sympathy, increase the mischief by half-truths or even lines, and make a bad matter worse. If a thing is not important enough to take up with the person involved, it is not important enough to take up with anybody. Much of such gossip is only a means to greater self-importance. Sometimes we are bored and want to create an "incident," so we blow up a small thing into something great, and talk about it widely. It would be a good thing if every one of us made a vow that we would never pass on a criticism of another person without having first made an honest try to clear it up with the person immediately involved. For what we have, even in so-called Christian families and groups, is a lot of human relations that will not bear much looking into. They are not founded upon loyalty and truth, but upon having managed and manipulated the other person with what we like to call tact. This is as true between groups as between individuals. If you want a really good spiritual exercise start praying about the unrealities and dishonesties and double talk in your human relationships; and go and repair them by "speaking the truth in love."

## II

How can one do this? What does "love" for people really mean?

Love means reality in relationships. It means being aware of people; it means caring about them; it means concern for them. The degree of personal warmth in relationships will vary, of course. We feel drawn to some people, and not to others. This need not mean resistance or criticism or feud with those to whom we do not feel personally drawn as much as to others. I believe that literally no person ever crosses our path without its being intended that something should pass from one to the other. I believe there is no one for whom we should not feel Christian love, in the sense that we feel a spiritual and human concern about him, and are eager to help him in any way we can. We may see genuine faults in him, as he may see them in us. Christians ought to be in a vast, redemptive game to win and help as many people as possible, whatever their need. All of us fail in this, but it seems to me the only meaning of "love your neighbor."

Of course we cannot do this of ourselves. We work naturally by affinity and by emotion. Only God can help us to work by concern and by grace. This is why human relations must not resemble two dots at the end of a line, but two angles at the base of a triangle, with God at the apex. God must be "in" on every human relationship if it is to be right. Two things happen when God comes in on a human relationship: (1) we then refer everything to One who is perfectly just and sees the situation exactly as it is, and (2) prayer opens us to see the situation more as it truly is, helps us to melt out of it unyielding and unjust attitudes, and gives us generous and redemptive and fresh attitudes toward people. God lifts us up into a creative and dynamic expectation, very different from our natural sullen self-justification. Of course we simply cannot bring our bitternesses and our unforgivingnesses and our gossip and our angers before God when we pray, except when we ask him to forgive and to change these things. If when we come away from what we call praying we hang on to any one of these things, we simply have not prayed, and we know it. Prayer reminds us continually of our own faults, and it forces us to take a forgiving and redemptive attitude toward what we think to be the faults of others.

Does this mean we simply slump down into the universal human failure—they sin, we sin, and so it's all hopeless? Of course not! To love people means that we long for them to have God's best, to belong to God, to serve him and trust him and enjoy the life he gives to believing people. To see a fault in them, or for them to see one in us, is only to recognize how badly we both need help from God. But we do not think we are hopeless—why think they are? Love always works for other people's redemption, not for one's own rights. Wherever and whenever I fight for "my side," as against the real truth—however unwelcome or hostile to my ego this may be—and if I can never vote against myself, I am really a traitor to God, humanity, and myself. All progress begins in a love for people and a love for the truth which is bigger than any man's ego or interests. To "bring a person into the Church" is not to get him to join an Episcopal or Presbyterian or Roman Catholic club to which we happen to belong; it is to draw him into a society of sinners who are learning to be honest about their own sins, and asking God for help to overcome them. If he knew that we were aware that we were first, last, and all the time genuine sinners, ever standing in the need of God's forgiveness and renewing grace, he would be much more inclined to link up with us. But do we feel this about the church, or do we feel we are among the best people in town because we come? And if we are sinners and know it, does it make us hopeless or expectant? Is our sin greater than the Lord who saves us from sin? Which bulks bigger in our actual thinking? We need to get all our human relations up into the presence of Christ, and let him judge of them, and let him remake them.

## III

We need to be Christian and redemptive in our attitude toward groups of people as well as toward individuals. We Christians are set to redeem all mankind, "them that are far off and them that are nigh," i.e., people in Africa and people in America. Will you tell me how you expect to draw God's ancient people, the Jews, to more openness toward the gospel when you live with dislike of them in your heart? Will you tell me how you expect to draw the great Negro population of this country, all of them brought here by the cupidity of white men, into one great fellowship, when you persist in thinking of them as inferior persons? Booker T. Washington inferior? George Washington Carver inferior? Take care what you say! You cannot find one whit of race prejudice in the New Testament under which to hide your own. You had better smoke it out, and call it the sin that it is, and change your heart. Elton Trueblood says:

Every white man who violated, in years past, the principle of the innate dignity of every human being by saying "Boy" to a Chinese man, was helping to build up the fierce hatred which finally has burst upon us with such apparent unreason.

I saw that with my own eyes in old Peking thirty-seven years ago. I saw the stupid representatives of British and American business failing in common humanity and courtesy—let alone in Christian love. They helped us lose Asia. You had better look to whether your own attitudes are helping us lose the rest of the world! Nobody wants "tolerance." I don't want to be "tolerated." I want to be understood as a human being, and treated as one. That's what every man wants and deserves. When we recognize characteristic faults in races—and perhaps they have them—let us face it also that superiority, arrogance, and complacency constitute our sins as a white race.

We shall learn one day that "getting along with each other" is more than a capacity to adapt; it is so bringing to bear the power of love and of prayer on human relations that they are changed. God does the changing; we let it happen by asking God to take the wrong attitudes from our hearts and give us right ones, and seeking to draw them also into this wonderful stream of power which is God's grace and our faith. We need an objective in our human relations, else we shall think them successful because they merely coast along happily. Every human relation needs the third party which is God to keep it real and loving and honest. This is true of our family, our friends, our business associates. Relationships become quite new when God comes into them.

Recently I saw it happen again—a young couple devoted to each other, but feeling their lives had come to a kind of dead end. They lacked purpose and zeal in living. Life was mostly problems. There was an in-law problem; there was the problem of aimlessness; there was the major problem of no God in the daily living. They surrendered these problems—and themselves—to God, and then stepped into the stream of God's love and purpose together. This is only a start. It needs sustaining, and they have begun a spiritual discipline which will sustain it. The old problems will still confront them, but there is a new power in which to meet them. Everybody will soon see the difference which Christian conversion makes.

# 17

# EQUAL—UNDER GOD

### Duke K. McCall

WOULDN'T IT BE TERRIBLE IF ALL MEN WERE EXACTLY EQUAL IN all of life's relationships? There would never be another baseball game, for all nine men would want to play the same position. Still worse, the score between the two teams would always be a tie.

Would it not be terrible if all men were exactly equal in taste? Every home, both inside and out, would look like every other home. And every young man in a community would propose to the same girl, and she would say yes to every young man.

Imagine the economic confusion in our country if everyone were qualified for the same job. Either nothing would ever get done or else 99 per cent of us would become round pegs in square holes.

Equality as an absolute standard on this earth is impossible. What most of us want is equality at some specific point; that is, we want to be equal in economic advantage with other individuals or groups, or we want to be equal in social privilege with another class of people, or we want to be equal in prestige or power or political opportunity with other persons.

The biblical explanation for the differences and divisions among men charges this disaster to human pride. In Genesis we read that the people of earth said, "Come, let us build us a city, and a tower, whose top may reach unto heaven, and let us make us a name." They state the reason for their mighty effort in the words, "Lest we be scattered abroad upon the face of the whole earth." Then God, taking notice of their impious efforts, comments, "Behold, they are one people, and they have all one language; and this is what they begin to do" (11:4, 6 A.S.V.).

When men were equal to one another they sought to become equal to God, but God turned back their pride upon themselves to their confusion and to the confounding of their purpose. The tower which was to reach unto heaven became the tower of Babel, and the symbol of the unity of mankind built by man's strength has become the byword for confusion and failure.

## I

Human pride still makes it difficult to discuss, much less to do anything about, the inequalities among men. The generally accepted phrase for soothing our consciences without coming to grips with the issue is "equality of opportunity." But we do not face the question: Equality of opportunity for what and with whom? I have a bachelor friend who says, "I can marry anyone I please." If your disbelief in his boast is expressed in a raised eyebrow, he will add, "Unfortunately, thus far I have never found anyone I pleased." Most of us would have to say, "I have the opportunity to work for any firm I please for any salary—if I please those for whom I work."

Today there is little equality *within* the races and even less *among* the races anywhere in the world. With or without legislative consent, human pride finds its own method of expression. The ideal of absolute equality, even of opportunity, appears unobtainable, although that makes it no less an ideal. And the matter is confused by some who seek to secure the unobtainable while others fight to prevent the inevitable. As in the days of the tower of Babel, the issue of equality has become an instrument of pride to provoke our people to division.

Regardless of the terms in which equality may be debated in other arenas, Christianity proposes to ignore the relative historical achievements and standards of men in order to raise all men into the equality of fellowship as children of God. It was this Christian equality which Thomas Jefferson had in mind when in the Declaration of Independence he wrote: "We hold these truths to be self-evident: that all men are created equal; that they are endowed by their Creator with inherent and inalienable rights; that among these are life, liberty, and pursuit of happiness."

The word of God recognizes that there are differences among men even in his service, for Paul says, "And he gave some to be apostles; and some, prophets; and some, evangelists; and some, pastors and teachers" (Eph. 4:11 A.S.V.). These differences and all others, however, are dissolved in the presence of God where "there is one body, and one Spirit, even as also ye were called in one hope of your calling; one Lord, one faith, one baptism, one God and Father of all" (Eph. 4:4-6 A.S.V.).

The recognition that absolute equality is to be found only at the throne of God lays a heavy responsibility upon the churches of God to represent him in his attitude toward the inequalities of life's actual experience. The churches must will so to transform men as to make it possible for the will of God to be done on earth as it is in heaven. In the relations between labor and management or the relations between members of the different races—in whatever area of economic, social, or political life—inequalities are always grounded in injustice, and the members of Christian churches must speak the disapproval of God.

## II

The church of Jesus Christ belongs to no class or race. As the instrument of God it must take as the clue to its course the nature of its God. First, the church must consecrate and sanctify itself to the ideals of a transcendent God. Men who seek God do not poke and putter in the muck and mire of the world; they lift their eyes unto the heavens. If, seeking worldly gold and glory, men come upon the church engaged in the same pursuit and covered with the stains of the world's standards, they are likely to ascribe little value to the church. Christ said to his church, "They are not of the world, even as I am not of the world" (John 17:16 A.S.V.)

Jesus Christ as the revelation of God taught and lived an infinite idealism which finite men with their bodies and souls scarred by sin will never attain, and the church for that reason accommodates its ideal and efforts to the abilities of men, thereby accusing Jesus of being a fool when he said, "Be ye therefore perfect, even as your Father which is in heaven is perfect" (Matt. 5:48). No social or economic or political system will ever attain to the full Christian ideal; consequently the church must rise above them all so that no relative historical achievement may become the basis for moral complacency.

Individual members of a church will inevitably conform to and co-operate with systems of their choice, but the church must fearlessly criticize the inadequacies of each while seeking to reflect the kingdom of God. Transcending earthly ideals, the church's fellowship should be a solvent for the most serious animosities. As transcendent it may minister to both overprivilege and underprivilege, even while opposing all special privileges as a denial of brotherhood.

But God is not only transcendent, he is also immanent. A church which is content to broadcast pious phrases to a world hurtling through space with chart confused and compass lost is a church which has forgotten its Master's message to the world. He spake truth who wrote:

I am far within the mark when I say that all the armies that ever marched, and all the navies ever built, and all the parliaments that ever sat, and all the kings that ever reigned, put together, have not affected the life of man upon this earth as powerfully as has that one solitary life.[1]

Who killed the monsters splashing in prehistoric swamps? No one. The climate changed, and they died. Jesus did not take up arms against the dragon of some evil system. He changed the climate by completely changing men. He did not just reform men; that would have been putting new wine into old skins. His message was not of a new look, but of a new birth which changed every point of reference in the individual's life from self to service in the name of God. The church of Jesus Christ can participate in all the turmoil and tension arising from the inequalities of men only by preaching and teaching a new birth in which a completely new spiritual being is born. Christians should not be a sort of centaur with the personal morality of God and the economic and social and political ethics of the devil.

[1] James A. Francis.

## III

Let us apply these convictions to the inequalities which exist between the white and Negro citizens in America. The following charter of Christian principles, which was accepted by the Southern Baptist Convention of 1947, "should be acceptable to all who are the children of God":

1. We believe in the Lordship of Christ: in order to act in his name in social relations we must love our neighbors, including our Negro neighbors, as ourselves.

2. We believe in the Holy Spirit: since the day of Pentecost he has been breaking down middle walls of partition between races and alien groups and teaching men of open heart to keep the unity of the Spirit in the bonds of peace.

3. We believe in the Bible as the word of God: in it is our authoritative summons to practice justice towards all people of all races.

4. We believe in the dignity and worth of the individual man: irrespective of his race or position he has the right to develop in the measure of his divinely given capacity and to share in just measure the blessings of our Father's world.

5. We believe in the fellowship of believers: a relationship which forbids us to allow worldly patterns of prejudice to drive a wedge between us and our Christian brothers of other races.

6. We believe in the principle of democracy in government: in application it entails the recognition and defense of the natural and constitutional rights of all citizens irrespective of their origin or racial inheritance.

"These doctrines, which must commend themselves to every conscience, impel us to the observance of the following principles of conduct:"

1. We shall think of the Negro as a person and treat him accordingly.

2. We shall continually strive as individuals to conquer all prejudice and eliminate from our speech terms of contempt and from our conduct actions of ill-will.

3. We shall teach our children that prejudice is un-Christian and that good-will and helpful deeds are the duty of every Christian toward all men of all races.

4. We shall protest against injustice and indignities against Negroes, as we do in the case of people of our own race, whenever and wherever we meet them.

5. We shall be willing for the Negro to enjoy the rights granted to him under the Constitution of the United States, including the right to vote, to serve on juries, to receive justice in the courts, to be free from mob violence, to secure a just share of the benefits of educational and other funds, and to receive equal service for equal payment on public carriers and conveniences.

6. We shall be just in our dealing with the Negro as an individual. Whenever he is in our employ we shall pay him an adequate wage and provide for him healthful working conditions.

7. We shall strive to promote community good-will between the races in every way possible.

8. We shall actively cooperate with Negro Baptists in the building up of their churches, the education of their ministers, and the promotion of their missions and evangelistic programs.[2]

Some years ago three men presented themselves for membership in a Baptist church in Washington. One was a common laborer, another was a native Chinese, and the third was Chief Justice Hughes of the United States Supreme Court. As the three stood before the congregation for presentation by the minister for full fellowship in the church, the minister said, "Thank God, at the foot of the cross the ground is level."

Indeed there is hardly anywhere else in all of the pilgrimage of man where he finds the ground level save at the foot of the cross of Jesus Christ. We who have stood there should never think more highly of ourselves than we ought to think. But far more important than that is the fact that no matter who you are or what you are, personal salvation is provided upon the same terms available to everyone. God commendeth his love toward us in that while we were yet sinners Christ died for us. We all stand upon level ground about the cross to cry, "Lord, have mercy on me, a sinner." Then it is that "the Spirit himself beareth witness with our spirit, that we are children of God: and if children, then heirs; heirs of God, and joint-heirs with Christ" (Rom. 8:16-17 A.S.V.) .

[2] *The Southern Baptist Convention Annual of 1947*, p. 342.

# 18

# WHO IS BEHIND THE BROTHER-
# HOOD MOVEMENT?

*Robert E. Goodrich, Jr.*

Scripture: Acts 10:9-35

EACH YEAR BROTHERHOOD WEEK IS CELEBRATED IN HUNDREDS OF cities and towns across America. There are speeches and programs and movies in schools and clubs and churches. Newspapers take note of it editorially and national advertisers give space to it. All of the arts of psychology and selling are called into play to make the message of brotherhood reach every person in the country.

Many of the churches in America also observe a Race Relations Day, and others give special emphasis to human relations during certain seasons. Whether the observance lasts for a day or a week, it is meant to point up a spirit of brotherhood which ought to prevail every day in the year.

Who is behind this brotherhood movement? The question is common in some quarters because many Americans are persuaded that nobody does anything just for the good of it, or for his health! He must have an angle; he must be in line to profit by it somehow. He's trying to put something over on us for a purpose! Most of us do not differ from the little boy who saw a rainbow in the skies and immediately asked, "What does it advertise?" Well, is all this brotherhood business something the Roman Catholics are trying to put over? Or the Jews? Or the Negroes? Or maybe the Communists? They profess to believe in a nonprejudiced society. Could they, as the undercover sponsor of

142

this movement, be trying to soften us up? Who is behind the brotherhood movement?

Actually the question is rather crucial for all of us. Upon the answer may rest the validity of our claim as Christians. Of course, we are not really asking what organization is sponsoring it or what groups are underwriting it. Long before there was a Race Relations Day, or a National Conference of Christians and Jews, or a Good Neighbor Commission, brotherhood was troubling the hearts and souls of men. Who is it that just won't let the matter die?

Let's go back to the time when this movement really got its start in early Christianity. The story is told in the tenth chapter of Acts of an experience of Peter which caused him to understand the practical implication of something he had been professing all along. It may seem incredible that men could live in the very presence of Jesus and be so orthodox in their faith, and yet misunderstand his deeds and words so completely. But we might do well to remember that intolerance and persecution almost always manage to be "orthodox." The inquisitors and witch burners of every age can quote scripture and claim to be the true defenders of the faith.

So it was with Peter and the other disciples. Those first Jewish Christians seem to have been certain that they were God's chosen ones, that he belonged to their race and kind. This is what made it so hard for Peter to understand his vision, and harder still for him to answer the call to the house of that Gentile, Cornelius.

But it was a great awakening for Peter when he discovered that his God had spoken also to Cornelius. The Holy Spirit could move in the heart of a man of another race and background. And it was a turning point in early Christianity when Peter finally spoke the words: "Of a truth I perceive that God is no respecter of persons. . . . God hath shewed me that I should not call any man common or unclean. . . . In every nation he that feareth him, and worketh righteousness, is accepted with him" (Acts 10:34, 28, 35).

The brotherhood movement was under way. Who was behind it? Who was it that spoke to Peter and to Cornelius? The spirit of that living God who is maker and ruler of all men, God the Father

Almighty, maker of heaven and earth. And it is this same God who troubles our consciences and stirs our hearts in the name of brotherhood today.

## I

Who is behind the brotherhood movement? The God who cares about us all because we all belong to him, the God who knows his children one by one, and whose will is that not one of his little ones should perish. He is the God of individuals.

We do believe that God cares about individuals, don't we? How desperately some of us want to be sure of it. We want to feel that he cares about us not *en masse,* but in person. So Peter treasured this kind of faith. He had seen it in Christ. But it was a rude jolt to his pride when he discovered that "God is no respecter of persons," that he shows no partiality. God could love a Peter, but he could also love a Cornelius. Thus for Peter to have the comfort, he had to accept the challenge.

And so do we! It is marvelous to feel that my life matters to God and that I am important in his sight. But how do we understand that? The Bible does not say it. The scripture does not actually say that John Doe or Jack Smith or Mary Allen is important to God. It simply says that he cares about his children, one by one. The principle is put into phrases such as, "The very hairs of your head are all numbered" (Matt. 10:30). This statement, though personal, is yet broad enough to include every man upon earth. If I am to accept it for myself, I must understand that it has to do with you, and with the one who is different, the member of a minority group or race, anywhere, anyplace.

Behind the brotherhood movement stands the God who looks at you and at me, and at his other children too, saying, "These are all my children and I care about them."

It is odd that sometimes we can understand this provided those "other" children are far enough away from us, perhaps across the state line, or the continent, or the sea. Most of us know some missionary hymns from memory, hymns which in various words put such a thought as this:

> The pretty brown babies who roll in the sand,
> In a country far over the sea,
> Are my African brothers, and Jesus loves them
> Just as he loves you and me.[1]

We have sung words such as these. But when that one whom Jesus loves is too close at hand, we may then sing different words to a different tune.

In east Texas not long ago a little Negro girl was discovered to possess an extraordinary voice, maybe a great talent. Marion Anderson was once such a little girl. Friends made it possible for the child to go to the city to study. She was accepted by one of the best teachers. But the teacher was forbidden to have this girl in her studios, forbidden by a concern which would have been glad, however, to sell the girl a musical instrument. It is not unlikely that this concern would have been even willing to contribute money for her musical education, if only she had been far, far away.

So we become anxious to send the gospel to India, where men are divided by the pagan caste system and where there are places which are forbidden to the untouchables. We must send them the gospel and try to open their eyes to the fact that God loves every single one of them. But when it is close to home, it is different! Witness the fact that certain groups even within Christianity have sung with all their heart:

> We are God's favored few:
> All others will be damned.
> There is no place in heaven for you,
> We can't have heaven crammed.

Yet, behind the brotherhood movement is the God who cares about persons and whose love shows no partiality because of place or race. He wants us to understand that these others belong to him too. We must learn to see them not as cases to be handled nor as

[1] Copyright renewed 1936 by Margaret Coote Brown. Used by permission of Abingdon Press.

groups to be patronized, but simply as persons. "Stand up, Cornelius," said Peter, "for I too am a man . . . that's all."

A child was once telling her mother about her new-found playmate and how much they enjoyed being together in their backyard playhouse. With a troubled look the mother said, "But, dear, isn't that little girl a . . . Well, doesn't she have black skin?" The child thought for a moment and then said: "I don't know, Mother. Tomorrow when we're together, I'll look and see." Maybe it will be hard to enter God's kingdom until, childlike, we see others just as persons.

The God who cares about us all expects us to see others, close by or far away, as persons. And if we want the comfort of believing this, we had better accept the challenge of treating them as if he cares about them too.

## II

Who is behind the brotherhood movement? The God who cares about this American democracy of ours.

I do think God cares about America and wants to see our way succeed and live. After all, it is the only nation founded not upon race or geographical boundaries, but upon ideals and principles which largely came from the Judeo-Christian heritage. So I think God is troubling our hearts and conscience about brotherhood because this democracy could perish from the earth if too many of us are prejudiced and narrow and unjust. Democracy cannot exist on mere professions of faith. It must have the strength and power that come from living the faith.

Any honest reading of American principles reveals that we believe in the dignity and in the inalienable rights of every person. This has got to work out in America. The right to be different, without fear of consequences, and the right to stand up and be a person, without fear, are rights that must be protected. And not for our sake alone, but for the sake of mankind. The eyes of the world are upon us.

But as we seek to make progress toward the real expression of brotherhood in America, we must be on guard against something that is a perversion of tolerance. It is the feeling that, after all, there is no real difference in the various faiths. Some people already believe that since some people like one thing, and others like something else, that the only difference between the one and the other is that some people like this and some people like that. Such a perversion can lead to chaos and weakness, but not to brotherhood.

There is a tremendous and real difference in what men believe, and it does make a difference. It is never true that it does not matter what a man believes, as long as he believes something.

I am a Protestant Christian. I could never be anything else, because I cherish dearly the freedom, the intimacy with God, and the democracy of Protestantism. But I insist that the Roman Catholic Church, for example, be protected in its constitutional right to propagate and proselytize, and the right to win America if it can. When that church puts forth its best effort, it is not bigoted. But likewise, we have the right to claim the same for Protestantism—no more and no less. And we are not bigots when we put forth our best effort.

Brotherhood comes into being not when we are reduced to the level of the least common denominator, but when we rise above pride to grant and protect the rights of others. Brotherhood comes into being when each one, proud of his own heritage and faith, surrenders no convictions, but yet is willing to clasp the hand of another person to walk along a common road.

Philadelphia is known as the City of Brotherly Love, but I think that for me it will always be the City of the Chapel of the Four Chaplains. Four men made real the meaning of brotherhood as they stood on the deck of their ship, the *Dorchester,* as it sank within twenty-seven minutes after being torpedoed at 1:15 A.M. on February 3, 1943. Included in the official report is this statement: "With utter disregard of self, having given away their life jackets to four men without them, the chaplains stood hand-in-hand, praying to the God they served, for the safety of the men."

Four chaplains of three faiths. Daniel A. Poling, father of one of the men, has said:

Each man had a dynamic loyalty to his own faith. But these four became one in service, in sacrifice, and in dying. Standing shoulder to shoulder, braced against the rail as the waters rose about them, each in the tradition of his faith prayed to God the Father of us all.

This is the finest brotherhood. The perversion of it, the weakening of faith to the level of the lowest common denominator, or the idea that anything goes as long as somebody believes it, can never make America strong. Only that genuine brotherhood in which true and loyal to our own faith, surrendering no convictions, we yet find a unity of spirit and understanding with those of other faiths, can make America strong and preserve democracy.

## III

Who is behind the brotherhood movement? The God who lays responsibility on individuals. Brotherhood is a movement, and yet it is such a personal thing. Its realization must always begin in the hearts of persons. It must be found there if it is to be found anywhere. God puts the responsibility on persons such as you and me.

That is the way it was with Peter. It was a personal experience for him. God spoke directly to his heart, and regardless of the wider implications, for him brotherhood was a one-man movement. The responsibility was upon *him* to "call no man common or unclean." It was a one-man affair, and yet see what came from that one heart set right.

Perhaps we have tried to excuse ourselves by saying that the problem is entirely too big for us to do anything about it. That is never true. It would be more correct to say that the problem cannot be solved without us.

After all though, in a matter like this, down deep we want it to be personal. We do not want anyone to solve it for us. We do not want someone to tell us that if we don't act thus and so, we are unchristian. We do not want someone to force conformity upon us. We want it to be personal. And it will be, for it is as individuals that we are judged before God. According to Jesus, we must answer for our own personal life. Were we moved with compassion for our fellow man in whatsoever state we found him? Did we care for him, minister to him? It is a personal matter. God is behind this thing, and we must answer directly to him in our own hearts.

Maybe this responsibility upon us means that we must rethink the question, and rearrange some of our ideas, become less positive and fixed in some of our thinking. Somebody has suggested that too many persons are positive about what they think because they just do not want to think any further on the subject. They have frozen their opinions, once and for all. But perhaps we should re-examine some of our positive positions regarding other persons or groups in the light of science, freedom, and Christianity.

Maybe it means that it is our responsibility to learn how to share the feelings of others, to get inside their skins and live there for a while, and to walk in their shoes. Thus may we learn compassion for the feelings and failings of others. A man came upon a group of six children who were all crying. When he asked them what the trouble was, one child volunteered the answer, "We have a pain in Billy's stomach." Perhaps we need to become child-like in that way.

Certainly it means that we have a responsibility to get our own hearts right before God. This would be to make our peace with such words of Christ as, "And other sheep I have, which are not of this fold" (John 10:16) and "Many shall come from the east and west, and shall sit down with Abraham, and Isaac, and Jacob, in the kingdom of heaven" (Matt. 8:11).

We may not be able immediately to force a change in a nation or a city, or even a neighborhood, but we can do something about our own hearts. Our own conscience can be made clear before God. We can "count no man common or unclean." God puts the responsibility on us.

I once listened to the pastor of a great church in a college town tell of his own experience. It was on a Race Relations Sunday that two Negro students from one of the colleges nearby visited the Sunday evening youth meeting in his church. That was a proper observance for the day. The trouble was that they returned the next Sunday evening. And that was all wrong! Before the evening was over telephones had been ringing throughout the membership. Something had to be done—and quickly.

The pressure piled up like a snowball. By Friday that pastor had to make his way to the college and to the dormitory room of those young Negro Christian students. He struggled for soft words in which to phrase his message: "I must ask you not to come back to our church. I beg of you to comply."

"As I walked back across that campus," he said, "I felt like hanging my head in shame. I even felt unworthy as a minister. And I prayed, 'Father, forgive me. Our Father, *our* Father, forgive me.' "

What should he have done under the circumstances? I do not know. Perhaps he did the best that he could do. What is the answer to the whole problem, all things considered? I doubt if anyone knows just now.

But this I do know. It was less than a month later that this pastor, in the prime of middle age and without previous warning, slumped at the wheel of his car one evening. His heart had stopped. And I am also persuaded that when he stood in the very presence of Christ, he could answer: "I did my best. My heart broke for others, others of your children. I did the best I could."

The God who is behind the brotherhood movement lays a responsibility upon us, as he did upon Peter. We may not solve all the problems or find all the answers. But we can at least answer for our own hearts. Brotherhood is a one-man movement, first of all. At least we can live as if "no man is common or unclean." We can understand that "God is no respecter of persons." We can show by attitude and deed that we believe that "in every nation he that feareth him, and worketh righteousness, is accepted with him."

# V

*Advent and Christmas*

# 19

# WAITING FOR THE SUNRISE

*Donald Macleod*

> When the fulness of the time was come, God sent forth his Son.—Gal. 4:4. They were all waiting for him.—Luke 8:40

MAXWELL ANDERSON IN HIS PLAY, *Wingless Victory*, PRESENTS A young sea captain who had sailed away from Salem, Massachusetts, about the year 1800. Seven years later he returned piloting his own ship, laden with riches from the Far East, and bringing with him his lovely wife, a princess from Malay. Instead of the heartwarming reception which he expected, the attitude of his relatives and former friends was forbidding and cold. They banded together in raising a wall of racial prejudice, religious intolerance, and social cruelty against this seeming affront to the traditional exclusiveness of their New England environment. Although this poor woman had abandoned her former superstitions and tribal customs, and had embraced the religion of her husband, these townsfolk kept her out of their circle and refused to make her one of their own. Finally, breaking under the strain, she decided to end her own life, and as the bitter tragedy closed and the curtain fell upon the final action, she cried, "God of the children, god of the lesser children of the earth, the black, the unclean, the vengeful, you are mine now as when I was a child. *He came too soon, this Christ of peace; men are not ready yet!*"

As you and I look at the story of the past two thousand years, what should we think of this poor creature's remark? Was humanity ready and waiting for the coming of Christ, or did he break in upon our human patterns too soon? The gaping and curious crowds, of course, were always waiting; they would wait with staring eyes for anyone who could work a cheap miracle or give them bread without toil or security without sweat. But aside from them and what they represented, was humanity in some universal sense waiting for "the flaming of his Advent feet"? Or are Studdert-Kennedy's lines the unvarnished truth:

When Jesus came to Golgotha they hanged Him on a tree,
They drave great nails through hands and feet, and made a Calvary;
They crowned Him with a crown of thorns, red were His wounds and deep,
For those were crude and cruel days, the human flesh was cheap.[1]

What of our own day? If nineteen centuries ago was too soon, what reason have we to feel that it would be any different today or that his coming would be more opportune? Suppose we were to take this question to the world of business, or politics, or international relations, or even to the modern home, what would we find? We would encounter people who still claim that "nature is red in tooth and claw" and therefore, in order to survive, a man must be not merely physically fit and strong, but must always look out for "number one." The gospel of the brave, holding up the arms of the fainthearted, or of denying one's life in order to realize its fullness, seems to make dismal reading in these times when brute force appears to be the only language this world will listen to or attempt to understand. The gospel that featured the second mile or the house built upon a rock seems innocuous and unconventional in a world that appears to believe in "an eye for an eye, and a tooth for a tooth." Surely we would be forced to discount this twentieth century as the least feasible time and say: "He came too soon, this Christ of peace; men are not ready yet!" Too soon to teach men that the road to humility is the way to spiritual leadership, power, and victory. Too soon to convince men that self-renunciation is the way to lasting success and moral maturity. Too soon to advise braggart men and belligerent na-

[1] From "Indifference," taken from *Sorrows of God.* Used by permission of Harper & Brothers.

tions that enslavement of others is treachery against the sanctity of the human soul, and deserves the wrathful vengeance of God.

We still have, however, the words of Paul and it was without any question or qualification that he said, "When the time had fully come, God sent forth his Son." And at that time, wherever Jesus went or whenever he appeared, apart from the irresponsible and wavering elements in the crowd, there were invariably those poor and spiritually beleaguered folk who were "all waiting for him." Indeed, it is the verdict of scripture that this was the time par excellence for the advent of the Son of God. James S. Stewart has said:

There is a tide in the affairs of God; and it is when that tide reaches the flood, when all the preparatory work is done and world conditions are clamoring for it and human souls are open, it is then, at the flood-tide hour of history, that God launches his new adventure.[2]

This is what is meant by the fullness of time. And this was *the* one great hour when as never before or afterwards could Jesus' coming be more fortunate, timely, and useful.

Notice for example how providentially the external conditions and circumstances helped in the preparation for this zero hour in the spiritual destiny of the human race. Into the Mediterranean world and its civilization had been poured the contributions of three national traditions: Roman, Greek, and Jew. For a hundred years before Jesus came the known world had been merely a loose aggregation of warring states and tail ends of decaying empires. Then Rome took over, and under the *Pax Romana* rivalry and discord gave way to unity and peace. Moreover, order among states meant freedom to move from one to the other. And hence, without passports or fear of iron curtains, the early messengers of Christ sped, bearing the good news to the farthest frontiers of the land. How could Jesus' coming be any more opportune than in circumstances such as these?

And there were the Greeks. What connoisseurs of beauty they were! What searchers after truth! These things found expression

[2] *The Life and Teaching of Jesus Christ* (Nashville: Abingdon Press, 1957), p. 16.

in their language, one of the grandest tongues of the human race. What a gift it really was. And very soon it became the unrivaled channel through which the great ideas of the gospel were proclaimed to generations who were waiting for more than order and beauty were able to give.

But there were also the Jews. They gave their peculiar consciousness of God, which through the chastening of the centuries had risen to loftier heights than with any other people upon the earth. They had indeed prepared the way of the Lord; and for them it should have been indisputably the fullness of time, as he came from the heart of their race and brought with him the promise to be the glory of his own people Israel.

He came too soon? Nonsense! This was the day and the hour. "When the fulness of the time was come, God sent forth his Son." And "they were all waiting for him."

For what then, in connection with Jesus, did men and nations wait? What difference has the glorious advent of our Lord made in the story of the human race?

I

They were waiting, in the first place, *for God to become real to them*.

But was not God real to these Hebrew people? Yes certainly, and on every hand they saw evidence of his flaming presence and sovereign purpose. And the psalmist, the sweet singer of Israel, wrote, "The heavens declare the glory of God; and the firmament sheweth his handywork" (Ps. 19:1). Yet there was the deep-seated feeling that, despite these magnificent affirmations, God was still in heaven and man was on earth; the Creator and his creatures were very far apart. And at times, when the destiny of the nation seemed shattered and the fondest patterns were broken, a man like Job would ask, "Wherefore hidest thou thy face?" (Job 13:24). But then, almost unconsciously, and in anwser to the very heartache of the race, prophets and seers sensed a figure taking shape upon the margin of the years, and Isaiah saw it as a little child whose "name shall be called Wonderful, Counsellor, The mighty God, The everlasting Father, The Prince of Peace" (Isa. 9:6). That person could not come too soon, for "they were all waiting for him."

For this Jesus, with his revelation of God as the Father of men —not merely of the Hebrew race alone, but of every lord and peasant and slave of the Roman Empire—and his proclamation that love, not hate, is the highest law of life, the world was waiting.

The late Arthur John Gossip of Glasgow has recalled that from 1530 to 1536, Bonnivard was held prisoner in the dungeon of the grimy castle of Chillon, where in the damp and dark he paced the narrow confines of his cell. But one day he climbed painfully up the wall to the tiny window from which he saw the lovely sky, the swiftly flowing river Rhone, the distant towers of Villeneuve. Then he dropped back into the cell, his grimy, living grave. But the sight from the window filled his soul with passion and he began to beat on the door and cry, "Oh, God, I must get out, I must get out, I must get out!"

That, in a sense, is a picture of the world and its need nineteen hundred years ago. Men had seen the God of the universe as it were through a tiny window. Then with a holy passion they yearned for a fuller disclosure of the reality of his being, and in response to their need God sent his Son. Did he come too soon? "They were all waiting for him."

## II

Now that God had become more real to men in Jesus Christ, a second desire was inevitably satisfied: *the loneliness was taken out of religion.*

I doubt if there is anyone who does not feel that religion is a lonely business in this twentieth century. It is so much easier to be one of a jolly, irreligious crowd than to be dubbed a kill-joy. Hence there is the tendency to throw principles overboard and to lose oneself in what everybody else regards as "the thing to do." The notes of adventure and moral indignation are soft-pedalled by those who have not the will to dare to take a lonely stand upon religious grounds.

Remember how on one occasion the eager and plaintive crowd had waited all night for Jesus, and was now pressing in upon him like a wave of the world's great heartache and spiritual loneliness. And among them there was a poor, diseased, and haggard woman, trying to reach the Master and being constantly pushed aside by stronger competitors, who stretched out a scrawny hand, saying, "If I may but touch his garment, I shall be whole." And suddenly, among the jostling crowd, Jesus turned and said, "Thy faith hath made thee whole" (Matt. 10:21-22). She was a miserable outcast of Hebrew society, but in response to her waiting soul, Jesus made her into a new creature and, what is more, he became the friend of her lonely heart forever.

What a lesson for those who spurn religion today because it is too lonely an adventure! Whenever your sincere faith and earnest desire are focused on Jesus, he turns to you and becomes your companion for life. How clearly does Phillips Brooks express this in that loveliest of Christmas carols:

> How silently, how silently,
> The wondrous Gift is given!
> So God imparts to human hearts
> The blessings of His heaven.
> No ear may hear His coming,
> But in this world of sin,
> Where meek souls *will receive Him* still,
> The dear Christ enters in.[3]

He comes to those who are prepared and waiting to receive him.

And you see from this how one question cuts sharply through all the clamor and tinsel of your Christmas preparations: are you prepared to receive him in this Advent season? I grant you that in certain sections of our world there never has been such a moral mess as there is today. Certainly God meant it to be better than it is. Yet, whenever any one man permits Jesus to come in on all he does and says and plans, not only is everything different in his life, but wherever he touches the world things are different. An adventure of loneliness! Only one man against the world! Yes, but with God in that man everything is different. Only you against the

[3] "O Little Town of Bethlehem."

world, but God's Son in you, and you can overcome the world! He did not come too soon to prove the integrity of this principle to men who were waiting to receive him.

### III

And now, finally, with God at hand in the person of Jesus Christ and as part of every man's destiny and plan, *each believer had something for which to live.*

One morning, several years ago, as I began one of my classroom periods, I called upon a Chinese student to lead us in our opening prayer. As long as I live, I shall not forget one particular line of his petition. He was a Christian gentleman if ever there was one, with his heart wounded by the fact that after repeated attempts to return to his own church in his native China, the Communists had slammed the door shut. And there in an American seminary, ten thousand miles from home, Mr. Chiu prayed, "O God, ever give us something to die for, for if we have nothing to die for, we have nothing for which to live."

Is not the problem with people in every age that they have nothing to live for? And simply because they have nothing for which to die. This was more true before Christ came than it is, or need be, now. In the ancient world the religious man of the Hebrew race had the Law of Moses, but who ever heard of a man dying for a code of laws? Or could a citizen of Rome die for a confusion of gods that appealed only to what was base and immoral in his own human nature? But, "when the time had fully come, God sent forth his Son." Then life became real and meaningful and great, because even at the cost of death itself, men would go on living for him.

A young Communist in China, as he was being led out to be shot, challenged his captors: "I am dying for Communism. What are you living for?" And by this defiant remark, he showed his ignorance of the roll of honor of the Christian Church.

He did not know Paul of Tarsus who said, "I am ready . . . also to die at Jerusalem for the name of the Lord Jesus" (Acts 21:13).

He did not know Henry Martyn who, in 1805, gave up a

159

brilliant career in mathematics at Cambridge and went out as a missionary to India, and who said to his critics: "I feel pressed in spirit to do something for God. Now let me burn out for God."

He did not know C. T. Studd who, at the age of fifty-two years, turned his back on home and country and went to lose himself for the sake of Africa, and who said to those who frowned upon his venture, "If Jesus Christ be God and died for me, then no sacrifice can be too great for me to make for him."

He did not know George Tyrrell, the Irish divine of the nineteenth century, who, when he was almost driven out of religion by controversy and discouragement, said, "But there is that Strange Man on His Cross who drives me back again and again."

All these have written indelibly across the pages of human experience that only in Christ is there Someone supremely worth dying for, and only in so doing have all men a reason for which to live. Jesus could not come too soon to tell us that!

Again the world draws near to the birth of Christ. Will this Advent be for you the sunrise of a new day? Will you by your prayers see God touching humanity as a little Child? Will your Christian faith lose its loneliness and become a venture with him for whom no cost is too great to die, and for whom to live is life everlasting? It must, if God's purpose for this world is to be realized. You will help to do it as you pray,

> O come to my heart, Lord Jesus,
> There is room in my heart for Thee.[4]

⁴ Emily E. S. Elliot.

# 20

# THE MYSTERY OF CHRISTMAS

*Harold Cooke Phillips*

For unto us a child is born.—Isa. 9:6

WE HAVE TRAVELED THE ROAD TO BETHLEHEM SO OFTEN THAT it is for us a familiar journey. But we can never exhaust its meaning. Though it is unlikely that we shall see anything along the way which until now has escaped our notice, yet the things we see are so basic that we do well to keep them always in view. There is a familiarity that breeds contempt. Never is this true of the Christmas story. This is a familiarity that awakens interest, heightens hope, and strengthens faith. May our journey this year be guided by the words of the prophet Isaiah: "For unto us a child is born."

These prophetic words, as the Christian church believes and teaches, have been fulfilled in the birth of Christ our Lord. The divine significance of his birth has inspired not only the theology of the church, but its most deeply moving music. We are always thrilled with Handel's *Messiah* as the chorus sings exultantly, "For unto us a child is born, unto us a Son is given."

This was an unusual child. The stories of his birth, marked by singing angels, adoring shepherds, wise men who came to worship him guided by a star—whether they be the poetic pictures of consecrated imaginations or historic facts—are the most beautiful and haunting ever told about the birth of anyone. We know he was an unusual child because he became an unusual man. Kenneth Scott Latourette, renowned historian, says that no life ever lived on this planet has been so influential in the affairs of men. And how true that is! The continuing influence of his life

161

comes from the fact that through him God has given us the fullest revelation of his nature, his will, his purpose for mankind. Let us recall three truths which grow out of this revelation.

## I

For one thing, we are impressed with the fact that so extraordinary a life could have come to us in such ordinary fashion. What seems more ordinary or commonplace than the birth of a baby? Hundreds of thousands are born every day and in all parts of the world. Two of the New Testament writers, Matthew and Luke, seemingly could not believe that a child born as other babies are born could have accomplished what Jesus did. God must have used some extraordinary means to produce so extraordinary a person. And so they said that Jesus was born of a virgin, conceived by the Holy Spirit.

But it is significant that neither Mark, John, Paul, nor any of the other writers of the New Testament mention his miraculous birth. Does their silence suggest that they thought this child was born as any other child is born? If this be so, did they want us to see that there is something potentially extraordinary about the things we take for granted? Be that as it may, there can be no doubt of the fact that God came in One who was made "in all things . . . like unto his brethren" (Heb. 2:17) , and has made us see even "the least of these my brethren" (Matt. 25:40) in a way not possible until he came.

This new dignity, wonder, and meaning that Christ has brought to our common human life cannot be explained merely by a miraculous birth. Indeed one is impressed with the fact that the Master refused to rest the validity of his God-appointed life and ministry on the miraculous. At his temptation he would not convert stones into bread nor leap from the pinnacle of the temple. His contemporaries sought for a "sign," something out of the ordinary that would convince them of his messiahship. He gave them none. Perhaps he did not because he wanted us to see God not only in the esoteric, but in the orderly and everyday experiences of our lives.

In our home relationships, for example, nothing seems so ordinary as a mother and her baby. Yet "The Madonna and Child" and "The Holy Family," immortalized in art, should be a constant reminder of the meaning of God to our homes. In the coming of Christ to a human family God has indeed transformed and ennobled the familiar relationships of the home. It might not be inaccurate to say that this is something unique in the Christian religion. None of the other religions of the world, so far as I am aware, identifies its origin so completely with the family. Their founders appear as mature men. We see them, if one may so say, as birds full-feathered, gone out of their nest and on their own. Christianity is an exception. It begins in the nest, a babe in a manger. Moreover, in our Christmas carols we sing not only about the Christ child, but also about Mary, Joseph, and the manger rude and bare. Christianity is the one religion rooted in a unique way in the family. In a certain sense it would be true to say that ultimately its roots spring not from the church but from the home.

This, as it seems to me, is a fact of far-reaching significance. If we really grasped it and lived it, how our home relationships would be transformed! The coming of Christ to us through human flesh has elevated and sanctified man's sex life. It has given spiritual meaning to the biological processes of nature. "What God hath cleansed, that call not thou common." (Acts 10:15.) There is a strong word in Paul's epistle to the Corinthians: "Do you not know that you are God's temple and that God's Spirit dwells in you? If any one destroys God's temple, God will destroy him. For God's temple is holy, and that temple you are" (I Cor. 3:16-17 R.S.V.). Christ was born to teach us that. Immanuel—God with us—shows us how changed and how meaningful life becomes when we realize it bears the mark of God upon it.

## II

There is another truth suggested by the birth of this child. His birth reminds us of the unpredictable possibilities that may be hidden in the most unpromising circumstances. The birth of Jesus was an event which, down the ages, prophets had foretold and for which men had looked expectantly. And now they come to "see this thing which is come to pass" (Luke 2:15). And what do they see? "A babe"—not "the babe"—"wrapped in swaddling clothes, lying in a manger" (Luke 2:12). The prophet said, "His name shall be called Wonderful, Counsellor, The mighty God, The everlasting Father, The Prince of Peace." (Isa. 9:6.) But there was nothing in what the adoring shepherds or the wise men saw to give the slightest inkling of all this. They saw a little baby; as far as eyes could see, no different from any other Hebrew child.

What an unimpressive discovery! What an unpromising fulfillment to man's long cherished hopes! The first worshipers may well have pondered: Is this the end of our quest and is the promised deliverer—for whom we have waited, prayed, longed—a baby, symbol of simplicity, humility, weakness? Ah, but this child was born to remind us how much can come from how little, and what unpredictable possibilities may lie in most unlikely places or people.

This should help us to correct our judgments. Too often we are impressed by earthquake, wind and fire, the noisy, the boisterous, the big and bizarre; but miss the still small voice, the sound of gentle stillness. Yet more often than not, as history shows, events which have seemed too trivial or unimportant to be mentioned have been freighted with world-shaking possibilities of which we never dreamed.

Consider the Exodus. The flight of the Israelites from Egypt was one of the turning points of history, yet Egyptian records of that time make no mention of their departure. Why should anyone be impressed by the running away of a handful of slaves? This was regarded as an incident too trivial to be recorded. But as we now know, like the helpless baby lying in a manger, that proved to be a mighty act of God. For those slaves who went away unnoticed and unrecorded were destined in the providence of God to be the instruments of his purpose. But for them we would not worship our God today.

So with the birth of our Lord. This greatest event, which stands like a watershed in history, passed unnoticed. The busy world of his day went about its business as though nothing had happened. The late Archbishop of Canterbury, William Temple, wrote:

> I don't know what Augustus was doing that night. . . . No doubt [whatever he was doing] he and everyone about him thought it very important. If an angel had come to him instead of to the shepherds and had said, "Leave all this alone; it does not matter; nothing matters to-night except the fact that a poor woman has had a baby in a stable" —Augustus and his courtiers would have thought a lunatic was playing a practical joke on them.[1]

Surely there is much we should learn from this. It is so difficult for us to realize that the headlines we see blazoned forth in our newspapers are, with notable exceptions, never happenings of first-rate importance. Such are always "spiritual events which are known only by their results." God does not seem to go in much for publicity. "Thy Father . . . seeth in secret" (Matt. 6:4).

Christmas, then, reminds us that we may be woefully misled if we evaluate life by its size, its noise, its pomp. We are wont to forget this. It seems to us that the important matters today are related to bombs and guided missiles and atomic warships; or to some spectacular social event that sends news-hungry cameramen hurrying from all parts of the world; or to some atrocious and shocking crime that makes newsboys yell their heads off as they display their headlines. These are the big, important events. So we are wont to think. Meanwhile there may be some babe lying in a manger, or some movement, some idea, some vision that stirs men's souls—unnoticed and unpublicized—that will live on and do its creative work when the tumult and the shouting dies.

Only a babe in a manger. Ah, we cannot predict what might happen when a child is born. We can never calculate the spiritual possibilities which inhere in a life God gives. "What manner of child shall this be! And the hand of the Lord was with him." (Luke 1:66.) The hand of the Lord is upon every child born into the world. But God's hand upon the child, his purpose and

[1] Quoted in Ernest Fremont Tittle, *The Gospel According to Luke* (New York: Harper & Bros., 1951), p. 12.

will for him, are mediated through our hands, our guidance, our instruction, our example. To try to bring out the divine purpose of life is surely our primary responsibility when "unto us a child is born."

Not only the manner of Jesus' humble birth, but the quiet yet constructive method of his ministry made his contemporaries doubt the validity of it. Even John the Baptist, his forerunner, doubted. "Art thou he that should come? or look we for another?" (Luke 7:19.) The answer of Jesus to this brave soul languishing in his dungeon must have been anything but reassuring. "Go . . . tell John what things ye have seen and heard." (7:22.) And what were those things? Well, all about blind men seeing, the deaf hearing, the lame walking again, the poor hearing the good news. But these were not spectacular things. They were not sufficiently impressive. They were not the things which the Messiah was expected to do.

This is evident from the prophet's picture of the Messiah. John described him as one whose

winnowing fork is in his hand, and he will clear his threshing floor . . . the chaff he will burn with unquenchable fire. . . . Even now the ax is laid to the root of the trees; every tree therefore that does not bear good fruit is cut down and thrown into the fire. (Matt. 3: 12, 10 R.S.V.)

That would make sense. People would have no doubt of the power of God used in such a forthright and dramatic fashion. The axe! you could hear the trees crashing. The fire! you could see the roaring flames reaching upward. By such vivid, impressive evidence of his judgment God would make his presence and his message real to men.

That the God whom Jesus came to reveal is a God of judgment, history plainly shows. But Jesus came to reveal the still deeper truth that God is primarily a God of love and mercy. The symbol of God he has left us is not an axe but a cross, not a symbol of physical power but of redemptive love. The Cross, however, did not impress his contemporaries. To the Jews it was a "stumbling-block" and to the Greeks "foolishness." Yet in the providence of

God this very thing, a cross, is for us a revelation of power vastly greater and more enduring than are the explosions that rock the world. But it does not make headlines. As Lecomte du Noüy writes:

The Roman patricians of the year 33, the philosophers, and the intellectuals would have been highly amused if they had been told that the unknown young Jew, tried by the procurator of a distant colony, . . . would play an infinitely greater role than Caesar, would dominate the history of the Occident, and become the purest symbol of all humanity.[2]

To the patricians, the philosophers, and the intellectuals he was just another misguided fanatic paying with his life for his dreams or illusions.

Ah, do not belittle a baby lying in a manger. Do not miss the deep enduring realities because they fail to arrest the attention of a publicity-minded age. Truly, "God hath chosen the weak things of the world to confound the things which are mighty . . . and things which are not, to bring to nought things that are" (I Cor. 1:27-28).

Here then are two truths suggested by the birth of this child: In coming to us as he did, God has permanently enhanced the meaning of human life and has, moreover, made real its unpredictable possibilities.

### III

There is a third truth. Christmas would not be Christmas if it were not for the sheer wonder of it all! "His name shall be called Wonderful." "All who heard it wondered at what the shepherds told them." (Luke 2:18 R.S.V.) When one thinks of the Christian movement, which, like a river with many tributaries, not only covers the world but has changed it in ways beyond our knowing; and then traces it back till it narrows down, so to speak, to a tiny trickle—a peasant woman and a child—we might justly use the words of the Psalms: "This is the Lord's doing; it is marvellous

[2] *Human Destiny* (New York: Longmans, Green and Co., 1947), pp. 163-64.

in our eyes" (Ps. 118:23) . To think that all *this* could have come from *that!*

We live in an age in which men seek neat and precise explanations for everything. Indeed there are those who are prone to believe that whatever cannot be adequately explained by our scientific techniques is unworthy of explanation and belongs to the realm of illusion. One scientific writer has said, "Mysteries must give place to facts." We have the facts; all else is fiction.

It is heartening to realize that such heady dogmatism is not shared by some of our greatest scientists. One of them has said, "We should be so wise if we could really understand a worm." Said Albert Einstein, in oft quoted words:

The most beautiful thing we can experience is the mysterious. It is the source of all true art and science. He to whom this emotion is a stranger, who can no longer pause to wonder, and stand wrapped in awe, is as good as dead: his eyes are closed.

Christmas bids us open our eyes to the wonder of God.

> Child, thou bringest to my heart
>   the babble of the wind and the water,
>     the flowers' speechless secrets, the clouds' dreams,
>       the mute gaze of wonder of the morning sky.[3]

There is a type of wonder which is "the child of ignorance," and another which is "the parent of adoration," of reverence, and awe before the mystery of life. In *The Fountain*, Charles Morgan writes:

Knowledge is static, a stone in the stream, but wonder is the stream itself—in common men a trickle clouded by doubt, in poets and saints a sparkling rivulet, in God a mighty river, bearing the whole commerce of the divine mind. Is it not true that, even on earth, as knowledge increases, wonder deepens? [4]

[3] From *Fireflies* by Rabindranath Tagore. Copyrighted in 1928, and used by permission of The Macmillan Company.
[4] P. 383.

It would indeed be strange if "the world will never starve for want of wonders, but only for want of wonder." [5]

This child was born to remind us that life is bigger than our precise calculations and neat explanations. Life can be neither fully comprehended nor contained by them. Our little vessels can hold just so much and then our cup "runneth over." What spills over from our factual vessels is by far the most meaningful and creative aspects of reality. In it is all the mystery of God's love and grace. In it is the faith that we are not alone, aimlessly adrift upon a shoreless sea without chart or compass, but that God has come to us to make known his love and his eternal purpose in Christ. This "passeth knowledge." It is faith.

Surely it must be evident that our knowledge, great and valuable though it be, is proving quite inadequate. Man is imperiled today not by his ignorance but by his knowledge. This is because it is not just what we know about the world, but what we *believe* about it that is of primary importance for our life. Christmas bids us believe that God loves the world and through Christ would redeem it. This is "the wisdom that is from above" (Jas. 3:17). It "passeth knowledge." It is faith. It is to such faith in a God who "moves in a mysterious way his wonders to perform" that Christmas calls us. "For unto us a child is born."

[5] Gilbert Keith Chesterton.

# VI

*Lent and Easter*

# 21

# UNCOMFORTABLE WORDS

## David H. C. Read

> And they were in the way going up to Jerusalem;
> and Jesus went before them: and they were amazed;
> and as they followed, they were afraid.—Mark 10:32

IT's A HARD WAY GOING UP TO JERUSALEM. YOU MUST TURN YOUR
back on the lovely lake of Galilee with its still waters reflecting
the tumbling green hills, and the spreading trees at the water's
edge where in the spring a carpet of little colored anemones
makes a pattern excelling "Solomon in all his glory" (Matt. 6:29).
You must take the long winding path southward to the hills of
Judea, and finally you must climb slowly up into the bare and
forbidding mountains which surround the ancient city of Jerusalem. No more green grass; just barren ground strewn with
gaunt boulders that look as though they had been left over from
an untidy work of creation. No more soft waters and arching trees;
just the hard path among the rocks in an empty sky.

### I

"And they were in the way going up to Jerusalem." This is
the turning point in the gospel story. The Galilee days are over.
There will be no more happy crowds gathered on the beach while
Jesus speaks from the side of a little boat; no more fiishing expedi-
tions; no more quiet evenings in the villages around Capernaum;
no more nights of deep communion under the Galilean stars; no
more swelling crowds hanging on his words and jostling to touch
the hem of his garment. Galilee lies behind. And "he . . . set his
face to go to Jerusalem." (Luke 9:51.) There was no other way

to fulfill his mission, to finish the work his Father had given him to do.

Galilee—home, friends, beauty of hills and lake, a growing movement, a responsive crowd, the marks of success. Jerusalem—the frowning city amid the desolate hills, the threatening power of Sadducee and Pharisee, the huge and unreliable crowd of strangers, loneliness, betrayal, and the lurking cruelty of Rome. Both these places belong to the ministry of Jesus. And the season of Lent forces us again to consider his way to Jerusalem.

I say "forces us" for we unquestionably prefer to omit the Jerusalem part of our Christian faith. We have developed a Galilee religion which, however valuable it may be, is less than half of Christianity. I believe that if we can join this group of men as they were "on the way going up to Jerusalem" we shall learn something of those deeper elements in our faith whose symbols are not sunshine, placid waters, and success, but storms, darkness, a crown of thorns, and a cross.

Don't misunderstand me. The things of Galilee are an integral part of our faith, and the peace and joy of which I have made them speak belong to the true and final substance of our life in God. But I should betray the Bible and be false to the testimony of the gospel if I claimed that they can be reached by any detour that circumvents that Jerusalem of suffering and stress.

> It is the way the Master went—
> Should not the servant tread it still? [1]

## II

"And they were in the way going up to Jerusalem; and Jesus went before them: and they were amazed; and as they followed, they were afraid."

These are uncomfortable words. We are right to turn to the Bible for comfort, but we are blind if we do not also see that it is full of uncomfortable words. "Comfort ye, comfort ye my people, saith your God. Speak ye comfortably to Jerusalem" (Isa.

[1] Horatius Bonar.

40:1-2), said the prophet of old, but that same prophet could at times speak most *un*comfortably to that same Jerusalem. "Why sayest thou, O Jacob, and speakest, O Israel, My way is hid from the Lord, and my judgment is passed over from my God?" (Isa. 40:27.) We have developed a selective method of Bible reading whereby I put in my thumb and pull out a plum and say "what a good boy am I," whereas we know perfectly well that some of the Bible plums taste very sour and bitter in our mouths and leave us feeling anything but good.

"And they were in the way going up to Jerusalem and Jesus . . . came alongside them and said, 'Cheer up, it may never happen.'" There are times when Jesus opens wide his arms to receive and to comfort all who are of a childlike spirit. But there are other times, and this is one of them, when the picture is very different, and Jesus stands before us, above us, beyond us in the radiance of a glory that shatters our self-confidence and brings us to our knees. Such, you remember, was the vision of the writer of the Revelation:

And he had in his right hand seven stars: and out of his mouth went a sharp twoedged sword: and his countenance was as the sun shineth in his strength. And when I saw him, I fell at his feet as dead. (1:16-17.)

This is the Jesus who comes to us in Lent to remind us that the Christian life is not "roses, roses, all the way," and to speak to us from that majestic depth where suffering is transmuted into love.

"And Jesus went before them." Can you see them moving up that rocky path to Jerusalem on that spring morning? Jesus is not with them. With face set in determination he strides on up the rocky path to meet his most deadly foes. Perhaps already on the horizon he can see a cross where some wretched rebel hangs a victim to the Roman power. And some distance behind come the disciples, in twos and threes, exchanging frightened glances, stumbling forward, tired, troubled—and as our text tells us— amazed and afraid.

## III

"They were amazed." Our Galilee religion has somehow lost this note of wonder and of awe. In a Lenten school, I have given a course of lectures with the title "Understanding Christ." I hope no one would think that we can ever fully understand. A great deal of my time has been necessarily taken up in recent years with attempts to explain and expound the Christian faith, and in particular, to elucidate what the Church believes and proclaims about Jesus Christ. Sometimes I have the feeling that it is possible to explain too much, to give the impression that by means of simple words and phrases we can make the person of Jesus plain and understandable to the ordinary man. In so doing we scale down the figure of our Lord to fit our puny minds, and, in the process, the glory fades and the mystery is vanished. It is as if we were to stand before the great rose window in the transept of Notre Dame in Paris, where the glowing, smoldering colors speak of the unutterable beauty of holiness, and were to say, "Let's explain it," and watch the colors drain away, the intricate patterns resolve into simple forms, and a clear, cold light of every day strike through a slab of plain cut glass.

Perhaps our modern training has robbed us of the capacity for this wonder and amazement. Yet this is surely one of the qualities of the child that Jesus commanded us to be. "Except ye . . . become as little children [except ye are able to be astonished, amazed at the mysteries and beauties of life, and at the most tremendous mystery of all—the glory of God in the face of Jesus Christ—], ye shall not enter the kingdom of heaven." (Matt. 18:3.) How is it with our sense of wonder? At Niagara Falls do we stand thrilled and astonished by this moving mass of water, this soaring spray with its glowing rainbow? Or do we say, "The precipitation of this volume of $H_2O$ from that height is bound to produce a fine distillation in which by refraction the primary colors will appear"? And do we stand before Jesus Christ confident that modern scholarship has placed him in his historical niche, and that his teaching can be easily codified and issued in digest form? Or do we kneel and say, "Thou art the King of Glory, O Christ, Thou art the everlasting Son of the Father"? [3]

## IV

"Jesus went before them: and they were amazed; and as they followed, they were afraid."

"They were amazed," yes, and "they were afraid." The way to Jerusalem should bring us back to a sense of amazement in the presence of the Son of God on that Via Dolorosa which ended at Calvary. But what about this fear? Are we to understand that the disciples were just plain frightened, scared—as any man would be—at the thought of the unknown dangers of Jerusalem? Or have we here again an element of mystery, a holy fear instilled by the figure of Jesus moving ahead of them up that rocky path to Jerusalem? And, most important of all, is there a place for such fear in the life of a Christian?

There is no easy answer to these questions. We can, if you like, say right away that a Christian ought not to be afraid of the future, ought never to be simply scared and terrified, provided we remember that there is a natural physical reaction to danger common to all men and women, an instinctive fear which, we are told, can act on our glands and blood stream so as to produce emergency energy in time of danger. In other words, faced with a man-eating tiger, we get from our fear power to come nearer the four-minute mile than ever before! This apart, fear in the sense of worry about the future, fear in the sense of distrust in our heavenly Father, is what Jesus condemned and came to save us from.

But did he condemn and does he want to deliver us from *all* forms of fear, from *all* forms of worry? Is there no "fear of the Lord" that is "the beginning of wisdom" ? On all hands today we are told that worry and fear are evil, and so, generally speaking, they are. But would it not be true to say that our real trouble is not fear and worry, but fear and worry about the wrong things? A man may worry quite uselessly about the possibility of having an accident, when all the time he *should* be worrying about his

[3] *Te Deum Laudamus.*

bad temper. A woman may worry day in and day out about her children's future, when she *should* be worrying about her terrible possessiveness. This matter is not as simple as it looks. Consider an extreme example. If a man came to my office and said, "I'm desperately worried, for I'm slowly administering poison to my wife and I'm afraid I'll be found out," should I answer, "My dear fellow, you mustn't worry, and you must cast out all fear"?

Do you see a sense in which a healthy fear, a deep sense of responsibility, a solemn care about our sins, *does* enter into the Christian life? "Perfect love casteth out fear." (I John 4:18.) Yes, but none of us has yet attained to perfect love, and there is a temptation to cast out all fear a little too quickly. Are you wholly comfortable in the presence of Jesus Christ? Is there no moment when his purity and love send a shudder through your soul? Then you have either reached the stage of perfect love, or you have not yet seen who it is who walks ahead up there to Jerusalem. The period of Lent gives us the occasion for a quiet and frank facing of this challenge and for giving him the opportunity to rid us *first* of our sins, then of our fears. Our trouble is that we want the fear removed and the sin to remain.

## V

"They were amazed; and as they followed, they were afraid." *But* they followed. This is the wonderful and glorious thing about the way to Jerusalem, about our summons to a fuller and deeper Christian commitment. In spite of our amazement and our fears, we are still given grace to follow. In fact, the more we are amazed by the majesty and the humility of Jesus, the more we are determined that this is the way, the only way for us. And the more we look into our own hearts and are ashamed at what we see, the more we are driven forward to seek the love that cleanses and inspires and casts out fear.

This Lord Jesus, in all the wonder and glory of his being; this Lord Jesus, in the awe-inspiring mystery of his Via Dolorosa, the Son of Man going "as it was written of him" (Mark 14:21); this Lord Jesus is the one who looks on us as he did on the ordinary men and women of his day and says simply, "Follow me." And the Lenten decision, the Christian decision, is nothing more and nothing less than this: "Lord Jesus, wherever it is, Galilee or Jerusalem; however it is, smooth or rough, laughter or tears; whenever it is, when I'm feeling prayerful and religious, or cold and uninspired—wherever, however, whenever, *I follow*." And remember when we make that decision in this difficult and threatening world, the whole forces of God are at our back.

# 22

# VIA DOLOROSA

## William Everette Phifer, Jr.

> And he, . . . bearing his own cross, to the place
> called the place of a skull, which is called in Hebrew
> Golgotha.—John 19:17 (R.S.V.)

THE NARROW STREETS OF OLD JERUSALEM WERE CROWDED ON
that unforgettable Friday of the Passover celebration. Merchants
from nearby villages, shepherds from the surrounding hill country, and travelers from far away mingled with the local populace
in pushing a rude way through the throngs of people. Jews from
near and far had gathered in the holy city of David that they
might celebrate the most important event in their religious
history. Here and there a street vendor shouted his wares, almost
unheard in the din made by noisy children playing in the filthy
streets. Here and there a sleepy donkey stood waiting patiently for
some master to goad him into unwanted action. Pushing, sweating,
discourteous people attempted to make their way through streets
that were not large enough to accommodate the swelling streams
of humanity.

Down one of those streets there came a procession to which
the Jews had become accustomed. Never did they bow their heads
in willing servitude, and always the threat of death hovered over
them, as time and again they revolted against the power of Rome
that lay like a choking yoke upon them. It was not unusual for
them to see a detail of Roman soldiers clear a passage through the
streets to make way for a death squad. So the fact that a group of
soldiers were surrounding three men with crosses on their backs
did not disturb unduly the people round about. At the head of

this column rode a centurion who was plainly contemptuous of all people who were not Roman born. His task was to make sure that the execution took place, and he would brook no interference. Cripples, children, old people were all alike to him, and all must get out of the way or be trodden under the hooves of his horse or run through by the swords of his men. It made no difference to him what happened to human beings who were not Romans and, therefore, deserved no compassion.

Nonetheless, the procession moved at a snail's pace. The soldiers found it impossible to keep step as they moved along. Shouting and cursing they tried to get their prisoners through this throng of people. The prisoners were the only ones who said nothing. They staggered along beneath the weight of heavy bars of wood, perhaps already stained with the blood of some former victim, for why should a cross be discarded simply because a man had died upon it? Use it again and again so long as it would bear the weight of its burden. It was hard for them to move along under such conditions, troubled by such thoughts as these men must have had, knowing that each step brought them nearer to death.

One of these three men was striking even in his evident state of near collapse. He had had no sleep, no food, no rest. He had been beaten and harassed until his wearied human body could stand no more. He staggered beneath the weight of his cross. Sweat poured from his body as he summoned the last resources of his failing strength in an effort to go forward. The rabble that followed the sad procession taunted him because he could not carry his cross unflinchingly. How little they knew of the real weight of that cross beneath which he swayed! Here and there a voice was raised in protest against a seeming injustice. "What has he done?" someone protested. "I have seen only kindness and mercy from his hands. Why is he being crucified?"

Another said: "He will not allow the Romans to do this thing to him. I once saw him speak to a man who was a leper and lo! the man was clean as a baby. He will march with these soldiers to the hill and there he will call down fire from heaven to destroy them all."

Yet another said: "Aye, friend, I too have seen what he can do. I was once with him in the village of Bethany and I saw him stand at the door of a tomb and call in a loud voice to a friend who had been dead for four days, and the man Lazarus came forth alive again. I saw it myself, and I know that it is true. He will never allow himself to be crucified."

Still another spoke: "But why does he let them do these things to him? If he has such power, why does he not use it? I do not believe that he can help himself. Who ever heard of a man who could save himself from such a situation refusing to do it?"

Others walked silently along with the crowd that was gathering about this procession of soldiers, for somehow men seemed to sense that this was not an ordinary execution. Women, their faces half-hidden by their veils, could not hide their grief. They had loved this man and they had seen his loving hands laid tenderly upon the heads of their children. Dispersed through the multitude were some of the disciples, whom he had chosen to be with him, but who had been too frightened to stay with him during the crushing hours of his trial. They walked slowly along, their heads still, their eyes filled with tears, their lips moving in silent prayers. They knew not what to do. Their Master was being taken from them and they had no power to rescue him.

But most of the crowd that followed had little interest in the matter. A mob had gathered because the magnetism of man's inhumanity to man had drawn these iron filings from near and far. These people had come to see a crucifixion and they were getting their hearts and minds in proper frame to appreciate to the full the animal cruelties of the hour. They taunted the condemned persons with all the imprecations they could think of. They tossed stones and pebbles at them to annoy them in their walking. Particularly did they vent their hatred upon the man who led the three victims, the man with the crown twisted from a long, thorned briar and pushed down upon his head until drops of blood mingled with the sweat of his brow.

Once as the procession halted for a moment, he turned to speak to his tormentors. Those who were closest to him shrank back from his gaze. It was not so much what he said—his words were

caught up in the babble of the sounds and lost on the winds—
but it was his look before which they quailed. There was something terrible in those eyes, as a man who had known agony beyond human words to express, yet also something so infinitely
lovely and appealing that his torturers fell back before him.
Then the procession moved on and the magic moment was gone.
Children's voices blended with those of their elders in shouting
curses at this man as he went forth to die. There is no question
but that this way from the judgment hall of Pilate to the top of
the hill called Golgotha will forever be known as Via Dolorosa.

What thoughts surged through the minds of the people that
day will never be known fully. Those who loved him were
stunned and horrified at the rapid pace with which events had
moved to this dramatic climax. They still looked for something to
take place that would relieve this gentle man of his suffering, but
each moment that passed decreased the likelihood. Those who had
never made a decision concerning him, but had seen the loaves
and the fishes and other wonderful things that he did, now
watched him as he mounted his last pulpit. Then shaking their
beards they joined in the derision of his enemies. The soldiers,
who cared nothing for all this, sat down beneath the shadow of
this dying man to gamble for the last vestige of his belongings.
But over it all there hung a question which even his enemies
asked silently to themselves: Why did this man die? Two of the
condemned had committed crimes, that was known, but this man
had really done nothing. Why did he die? Insistently we ask that
question today.

## I

First of all, Via Dolorosa was reality because Jesus was such a
good man. We have our little mottoes saying that virtue brings
rich rewards, and honesty is the best policy, and similar platitudi-
nous sayings, but actually we are forced to admit that these things
do not work out in everyday living to our material advantage. The
man who is dishonest ofentimes gets rich, while the honest clerk
labors for years at a pittance of a salary. The person who is virtu-
ous sometimes sees the procession of fame and fortune pass him

by with scarcely a nod in his direction. Jesus, who was incarnate goodness, bowed his head before the onslaught of Jewish hatred and Roman cruelty, and all of his goodness failed to release him from the bonds of suffering that evil forged about him. For his kindness he got a crown of thorns, for his gentleness he got a scourged back, for his love he got a cross too heavy to bear.

Such is not a very heartening thought. Why should there be any effort on our part to follow some path that leads in a twisted, tortuous manner through valleys lined with rocks of suffering simply because such a path is the one of goodness? It does not seem to pay very well in dividends. The answer is that all depends on what kind of person one wishes to be. But first of all, let us straighten our thinking. It is not an easy way with which Jesus challenges us. It calls to something deep within the soul and demands of us every ounce of manhood that we possess. If you do not wish to be a man and are content to be an animal merely satisfying appetites and desires as they occur, then you had better not attempt this Christian way. The artists who have painted Jesus as a weak-looking, emaciated, pale, anemic being have missed the true conception of him entirely. Herod was weak, Pilate was weak, Caiphas was weak, but not Jesus. Strength was all about him, and a portion of his inheritance always.

Does it pay to be a good person? It depends entirely upon the kind of pay that you want. Jesus had no earthly reward, but his name is more profoundly influential today than that of any other man who ever lived. Think of all the storms that have swept across the face of our world for the past nineteen centuries and one cannot fail to be moved by the fact that this man still stands as a monument to the satisfaction of right living. No weakling could have cast such a spell upon the ages. Only a man who had learned a secret deeper than any that men had hitherto had revealed could have pointed out such a way for men to follow.

Ultimately we find the problem devolves into a question of selfishness or unselfishness. The man who lives for the moment finds that his appetites can be met, his desires can be somewhat realized, and his hopes can be fulfilled. But there is a scant happiness to it all. For man was not meant to live like that, and no amount of the material serves to meet the deep-rooted needs of his spirit. These things do not satisfy, and he is foolish who thinks so. Alexander changed the map of the world, and died sighing for more worlds to conquer. Jesus changed the motives of men. Caesar pushed back a frontier, and died surrounded by false friends. Jesus purified and enlarged the faith of men. Charlemagne carved out a kingdom for himself, and died an embittered and disillusioned ruler. Jesus laid the foundation for a kingdom of righteousness and justice and truth. He still walks through the deserts of our living, and where we bid him welcome he changes them into fragrant gardens, enlarging their horizons and altering the moral climate. Yes, goodness crucified him, but I take my stand on that side, knowing full well that such is the only way for permanent happiness.

## II

Yet again, he was crucified because of the stubborn convictions of men. Judas, believing that this Man had tremendous power, attempted to force him to manifest it. Judas sold the Master not for greed—thirty pieces of silver was a paltry amount of money— and not even because he was disappointed in him. Judas sold Jesus into the hands of his enemies because he firmly believed that once the shackles of Roman authority were placed about him, the Master would call down fire from heaven and consume all his enemies. Judas had a stubborn conviction that he was right and that the way of Jesus was wrong. He followed his way, and the last glimpse we have of him is a body swaying wildly in the wind— lifeless, meaningless, hopeless.

From the safety of twenty centuries we heap imprecations of the most virulent sort upon the head of Judas. His was a despicable act and we find no excuse for it, even while understanding its motivation. But we cannot gather our skirts about us with complete disregard for our own shortcomings. We too have firm convictions that we are right about certain things and Jesus is wrong. We have read his words with seeming care, but we have dismissed them as being spoken to another age. He is a menace to so much that we like to do. Remember that ecclesiastical politician's of his day did not crucify him for preaching the love of God. They did not hate him because he proclaimed the acceptable time of the Lord. They did not persecute him because he pictured sublime ideas of heaven. They destroyed him because he over-turned the money changers' tables, because he challenged their strait-laced adherence to a set of regulations that served to enrich the rich at the expense of the poor, and· because he rebuked their bigoted patriotism and threatened their vested interests. They slew him because they had convictions that their way was right and that his was wrong for them.

Jesus still is a menace to those who would follow their own stubborn and stupid convictions as to the way that things ought to be done in this world. He has offered us a way of life and we have not been willing to accept it because we have been convinced in our thinking that we know much more about modern Occidental life than he, with his Oriental viewpoint, could ever know. If he really ruled our thinking and we gave over our convictions to his care that they might be molded in accordance with the principles that he laid down, what a different world this would be. If he was really the ruler, then war as a method of settling international differences by slaughtering large numbers of pink-cheeked boys would be no more. Our narrow, nationalistic outlook would be broadened so that economic interests would not always dictate our foreign policy. Our racial problems would sink into the background of an understanding that would sweep all else before the flow of its tide. Jesus trod slowly the Via Dolorosa because men were convinced that he was all wrong in his estimates of life and its values. May God forgive us that so often we have the same conviction.

## III

There is one further reason for that slow and measured tread up the hill of the skull. Jesus knew that this was the only way in which a race might be saved. Had there been any lesser way, the blood of the Nazarene would not have stained the cross. But this cosmic adventure of redemption was no ordinary event and it required no ordinary sacrifice. Jesus, the Son of God, was lifted up that he might draw all men unto him, because there was no other way for this salvation to be accomplished. The day became as night, but it was not dark enough to hide this deed. Jesus was telling mankind something about the heart of the universe, and as he laid bare its bleeding center it was seen to be love. It sounds like foolishness to the world, but the centuries have proved its adequacies.

In our sophisticated day, with its constant demand for reality, we meet oftentimes persons who refuse to accept this sort of a theory about the redemption of men. "Tell us more about it," they say. "How could one man dying upon a cross serve to bring all men into the presence of God in a clean manner? It doesn't make sense that this man could carry upon his shoulders the sins of the world." Men have been saying that for twenty centuries, because they do not like to face up to all the implications that are involved in its acceptance. But their words are as hollow echoes in the face of facts as they are. The mysteries of the Cross are insoluble, but they show certain indisputable facts to those who will heed.

Whatever we may say about the Cross and its difficulties intellectually, there is one thing that we must always allow, and that is its power. When the Cross lays hold upon a man there is some appeal about it that will not be denied and from which we do not escape, no matter how much we may think that we want to. It sends its searching roots into the very bottoms of our hearts and wraps them around those things that are fine and noble and good. Life becomes beautiful because the influence of the Cross of Jesus Christ shines radiantly in our experience.

Many times the fact has been alluded to that the man who wrote the hymn "In the Cross of Christ I glory, towering o'er the wrecks of time," Sir John Bowring, was the manipulator for the British government when the opium traffic was being forced upon China. It is practically impossible to believe that such a hymn could have been written by a man with such a despicable job. But that is not the whole of the story. Go back and read his life and you will discover that he was a man of generous philanthropy, of wide influence and usefulness, of high service between nations.

He had a black mark upon his career, but this Cross of Christ was strong and Sir John felt its power in an illustrious career.

Or consider the example of John Newton. He wrote, "How sweet the name of Jesus sounds in a believer's ear!" Who was John Newton? A slave trader who dealt in human lives between Africa and the slave markets of the western world. He held services twice each Sunday while the stench of doomed humanity rose to his nostrils from the hold of the ship. But that is not all of the story of the life of John Newton. Here is his epitaph which he himself composed:

John Newton, Clerk, once an infidel and libertine, a servant of slaves in Africa, was, by the rich mercy of our Lord and Saviour Jesus Christ, preserved, restored, pardoned, and appointed to preach the Faith he had long labored to destroy.

The Cross simply does not let a man go. It saves him. There is no other way!

Jesus still treads the Via Dolorosa! Sometimes we can almost hear him as he cries again, "My God, why hast thou forsaken me?" We know the fellowship of his loneliness, and yet we refuse him. We hear him calling, and yet we turn deaf ears to his pleas. He died for you. Isn't that enough? Isn't that enough?

# 23

# NOT MEANT FOR DEATH

*Joseph R. Sizoo*

THE HEART OF THE WORLD IS KNEELING ONCE AGAIN BEFORE THE moving story of the Resurrection. Like bells of hope, clear, resonant, harmonious, the song of the risen Christ rings over land and sea.

One of the amazing and hopeful characteristics of this confused and frustrated age is its increasing reverence for the Easter festival. Each year affection for it grows. This is one of the hopeful signs of the times. Easter has become humanity's day of jubilee. It is the one day whose sunrise is awaited by untold millions. Indeed, there are those for whom it is their only excursion into the spiritual world. The person who said religion has lost its hold on people must have died the night before Easter dawn. We know now that the history of the modern world began when angels in shimmering white announced, "He is not here: for he is risen" (Matt. 28:6). It is a day which puts a song in the heart, iron in the blood, and fires the flames of faith. If you were to take Easter out of the calendar, the bottom would drop out of the universe.

Gilbert Keith Chesterton once wrote, "A real Christian who believes should do two things: dance out of the sheer sense of joy, and fight out of the sheer sense of victory." Why is that so? What makes this day so profoundly significant for our times? What does it say to us in this hour of tension and bewilderment?

I

Easter is the story of a discovery, the discovery that Christ lives. He is alive in the world. It has taken one deep fear out of life, the fear of death. Have you ever thought how visibly disappointed the disciples must have been with the events of those last few days?

189

Calvary was to them an irretrievable disaster. Golgotha scarred their souls. It seemed like the closing of the book and the last good-bye. There was nothing left but to pick up the broken threads of life and walk back into endless loneliness. Betrayed by those he trusted, scourged by those he pitied, abandoned by those he loved, and with a scarlet camp mantle flung contemptuously across his shoulders, crowned with a crown of thorns, he carried his cross to an outlaw's grave. The setting sun held no vistas. He who had been born in a borrowed manger and rode to triumph on a borrowed beast was laid away in a borrowed tomb. Their last act of devotion was to prepare and anoint his body for burial. If they had thought he would rise again, they would have brought garlands and fruit. Not a single disciple believed he would live again.

Then out of the sepulchral gloom of the garden of the Arimathaean came the glorious song, "He is risen." They were not alone. He had walked back into their lives. Death had not changed him. His love had not ended; his compassion had not folded up; his forgiveness had not shriveled. Time and space had not changed him. He knew Mary by her voice, Peter by his faults, and Thomas by his doubts.

In the heart of the Easter story stands the deathless assurance that Christ lives, making himself available to our needs. We do not make our way alone through this world. As surely as he walked the dusty roads of Palestine, so surely he accompanies us on every highway. As surely as he gave sight to the blind and healing to the sick, so surely does he open our eyes to the spiritual world and heal the hurts of life. As surely as he stilled the storm, so does he calm the tempests which rage in our souls, and bring us peace.

Christ is not a memory, but a presence; not a figure in time, but a timeless figure. When doors close and life tumbles in; when the lamps go out and the lights begin to flicker; when hope no longer sees a star, and love no longer hears the rustling of the leaves; when horizons lose their crimson and skies become leaden; when it is touch and go—then comes a voice saying: "Trust me. You are not alone. Be not afraid. I live."

John Greenleaf Whittier wrote:

No fable old, nor mythic lore,
  Nor dream of bards and seers,
No dead fact stranded on the shore
  Of the oblivious years;—

But warm, sweet, tender, even yet
  A present help is He;
And faith has still its Olivet,
  And love its Galilee.[1]

And because he lives, we too shall live. In answer to the age-old question, "If a man die, shall he live again?" (Job 14:14) Easter declares, "As in Adam all die, even so in Christ shall all be made alive" (I Cor. 15:22). The souls of the righteous are in the hands of God. No torment shall touch them. When the heart cries out, "Father, tell us where they are," the answer comes, "In my keeping, night and day." Over the broken waves of life comes the golden glow, "He that believeth in me, though he were dead, yet shall he live: . . . whosoever liveth and believeth in me shall never die" (John 11:25-26). We shall see them again in that better country where the boatman with the silver oars takes us across the river that has no bridge; where the air is redolent with eternal spring; where we never grow old, never know pain, never know weariness; and where God shall wipe away all tears from our eyes. They have fought a good fight, finished their course, kept the faith, endured as seeing him who is invisible, bore the testimony of a good conscience; their robes were made white in the blood of the Lamb, and for them all the trumpets have blown on the other side.

And with the morn those angel faces smile
Which I have loved long since, and lost awhile.[2]

## II

But there is more to it. It goes deeper. Easter is not only the discovery that Christ lives, but even more important, it is the dis-

[1] From "Our Master."
[2] From "The Pillar of the Cloud," John Henry Newman.

covery that Christ triumphs. It takes out of life not simply the fear of death, but the fear of defeat. It holds before us not only the guarantee of endless living, but of victorious living.

What gladdened the disciples was not merely that Christ survived death, but that he conquered death. It was not so much an event in the physical world as in the spiritual world. Easter is not the story of a resuscitation, but a resurrection.

If Christianity had ended in a cross, we should never have heard of it. If it offered nothing beyond Calvary, it would be a religion of despair. If Christ had died and remained in a grave, then what Mephistopheles said to Faust would be true: "The ultimate value of everything is nothing."

Easter changed a martyrdom into a triumph; it turned a disaster into a coronation. On Good Friday the world said, "No"; on Easter Sunday God said, "Yes." There is no grave deep enough, no seal imposing enough, no guard powerful enough, no stone heavy enough, to keep Christ in the grave. The world learned for the first time that hate, violence, and greed are not the most potent forces on earth. Calvary does not settle the issue, nor close the book.

The political double-crossers who scourged him did not speak the last word; they only wrote themselves into oblivion. The crafty men who tried to push him out of the world did not speak the last word; they only dug their own graves. It was true two thousands years ago. It is still true. That is why Easter is the essence of everything that makes life worth living. It means that truth is more powerful than error; that principle is more eternal than expedience; that giving is more divine than getting; that sharing is more lasting than saving.

That needs saying today. We live in a badly frightened world. We seem like people who walk on streets which have no foundation, who live in houses which do not shelter, who eat food which does not nourish. Life has become so complex and complicated that we have become entangled by our own ennui. Columns of smoke rising from the smudge pots of despair are hiding the stars. All meaning has gone out of life. Many have made themselves

192

believe it doesn't matter whether they gain or lose, sink or swim, rise or fall, live or die. Clarence Darrow said to me one night, "Life is an unpleasant interruption of nothingness." Many believe that philosophy! A kind of irrationality rests upon our world. Issues seem confused. The age is full of misgivings, anxieties, and uncertainties. We have become fussy and panicky. We are slinking back into ugly moods, sour tempers, and bickering cynicism. Things seem to be getting out of hand. Despair is gnawing at the lute strings of life. Some are cynical, shrugging their shoulders and saying, "What is the use?" Many are already despairing of a new world before we have finished laying the foundations.

You will hear people say, "Good will is a wonderful thing, but it won't work; kindness is a supreme virtue, but don't expect anything to happen because of it; brotherhood is a golden dream, but only a dream; forgiveness is a hollow hope; hunger will always gnaw; pain will always prevail; disease will always ravage; ignorance will always have a toe hold; and the four horsemen of the Revelation will always ride."

To such an age comes the Easter festival. We can look class hatred, racial bitterness, and crass secularism in the face and say: you can't win. Evil hasn't a ghost of a chance. In the long run of history wrongdoing is a dead-end street. God is still God; Christ is still Christ. Love is the most omnipotent thing in the world. Issues in which God has a stake may be deferred and postponed, but they cannot be defeated. History is coming out somewhere. History belongs to God. I am willing to believe that many things happening in this world today are not in accordance with the will of God, but nothing happening in this world today can defeat his will. What holds the universe together is not chemistry, but spirituality; not blind chance, but eternal purpose. We are held by a love that will not be defeated.

The fundamental questions which every reformer, social worker, political leader—every sufferer for truth—must ask are: Is it worth while? Will anything come of it? The struggle for truth, freedom, justice, good will—has it a gambler's chance in this world? Here we are, seeking to live in peace and good will with all mankind. We want no one's land and no one's territory. I know we say it blunderingly—sometimes we blow hot, sometimes we blow cold. But in spite of everything and underneath everything, we want to live, let live, help live. Yet all this is evil spoken of and willfully misintepreted by some nations.

What is the answer? Patience. Lincoln was right. You can fool all the people some of the time, and some of the people all the time, but you cannot fool all the people all the time. One day when this insanity ends—as it will end—and the angels of their better selves get a chance, they will break through that iron curtain and welcome us in friendship. That may be difficult to believe, but it is infinitely more difficult to believe the only other possible alternative.

On Easter you hear the ageless assurance: There is no evil powerful enough and no hate bitter enough to keep the things of Christ in the grave. Truth crushed to earth will rise again. It may be postponed, but not conquered; deferred, but not defeated; defaced, but not effaced. To the man who thinks, life is a comedy; to the man who feels, life is a tragedy; but to the man who believes, life is a victory. The moral ventures you make, the costly loyalties you endure, the unrequited love you suffer, the holy dreams you dream are not in vain. Greed and hate are only illusions. At best they are like rockets displaying fantastic cascades of stars for the moment. But they soon fade and burn up.

Spires outlast spears; altars are more lasting than armament; freedom, truth, love, belong to the stuff of eternity. They are as invincible as light, as inviolable as sunbeams.

If we could lay hold of that assurance, turn it loose in the world, implement it in our time with courage, imagination, and vision, this bewildered age would have a new birth of hope. The Sermon on the Mount will outlast a blood purge. The Cross will outwit the hammer and sickle. Jesus Christ will outlive Karl Marx. Not Pontius Pilate, but Jesus speaks the last word. A man is a poor Christian who does not feel the steadying power of this story in his pilgrimage through the years. Take heart. This is Easter. Jesus Christ triumphs.

194

He has sounded forth the trumpet that shall never call retreat;
He is sifting out the hearts of men before His judgment seat:
O, be swift, my soul, to answer Him! Be jubilant, my feet!
　　　Our God is marching on! [3]

Over the tumult and tumbling of worlds and through the dilemmas and misgivings which crowd our lives and haunt our age comes the deathless assurance, "Alleluia: for the Lord God omnipotent reigneth" (Rev. 19:6).

---

[3] From "Battle-Hymn of the Republic," Julia Ward Howe.

# 24

# JESUS STANDS IN THE MIDST

*Paul Scherer*

Then . . . came Jesus and stood in the midst.
—John 20:19

THAT'S THE THEME, REALLY, OF THIS WHOLE RESURRECTION symphony in the Fourth Gospel. If we read any of it now on any of the more shallow levels of history, we misread it. One is deliberately refused the luxury of setting it down in the simple category of the past, and so in a sense being rid of it. That first morning in the garden Mary said, "They have taken away my Lord, and I know not where they have laid him" (John 20:13). Why do you think these little Christian communities scattered about in a hostile world cherished that story through the years? And this that came of it: "When she had thus said, she turned herself back, and saw Jesus standing, and knew not that it was Jesus" (20:14). The other story, about those men in the evening, hand-picked to upset things but huddled together now for fear, shut up with a memory; and Thomas, who called the whole thing nonsense when they told him, was only to be confronted himself a week later by that haunting figure of a man—"Then came Jesus and stood in the midst"—the words repeat themselves. And once more he said, "Peace" (*Shalom*), and called Thomas by name, and held out his scarred hands! It wasn't just something that had happened once—any more than that the whole Bible was just something that had happened once. It kept on happening—and whatever keeps on happening is hard to refute! Maybe even then you trudged back dispirited to the old routine tasks, as Peter did still later, up in Galilee. "I go a fishing," he said. Why not? It was all

196

over, wasn't it? And the others joined in, "We also go with thee." But there in the dawn stood Jesus on the shore, and "the disciples knew not that it was Jesus" until he gave them the old familiar sign: "Cast your nets!"

Now there's a pattern in all that, and I want to see if we can follow it through. As these stories unfold, there's always something about Christ's coming back from death that everybody likes very much—if that isn't putting it too mildly. So much so that you wonder now and then if our faith at this point isn't what a good many people say it is—a bit of wishful thinking! I'm sure that pulpits on Easter Sunday are as a rule full of everything about it that we like! And indeed half the Gospel does run that way. But I wonder if we're aware that the other half, so to speak, runs the other way? It keeps hinting at things about Christ's coming back that we don't like while both halves come to their point in this: that whether we like it or not, we have to do something about it. It's all there, I believe, in these last two chapters of John: the pattern of a past which is forever strangely present.

I

Let's be quite blunt then: What is there about the Easter gospel which says what we want it to say? A Columbia student once remarked of the sermons he had listened to in New York, that most of them left him thinking as he went out of the church, "That isn't true; but I wish it were!" Well, Thomas belonged to his party, and there's no counting the thousands in every generation that do. But it's a risk we have to run, here in the New Testament: the risk of coming to grips with what the disillusion that begets cynicism, and the cynicism that begets a proverb would insist on pronouncing "too good to be true"! Perhaps "too good not to be true" fits God's world better.

What happened that evening in the upper room, or wherever it was, and goes on happening, was what everybody there very much wanted to have happen. It was God's way of saying something that desperately needed to be said about this place we live in: that no matter how it looks, it's not the kind of place where you can finish off the Sermon on the Mount with a hammer and some nails. It isn't the kind of place where D. H. Lawrence can write in a postscript to Katherine Mansfield, "Don't worry, Kate; Jesus is a back number," and appear to be anything but incomprehensibly silly! A good deal more was going on under the sun than a "tale told by an idiot"; and death couldn't stop it. They needed to hear that—there under the roof behind the locked door. They needed to hear it in O'Neill's *Long Day's Journey into Night,* in Tennessee Williams' *Cat on a Hot Tin Roof,* and in Colin Wilson's *Outsider;* but nobody heard, so everything added up, act after act, page after page, to no more than the grin on poor Yorick's skull. It was "very early in the morning, the first day of the week," that God said "No!" He said *no* to the judgment hall, where they had tried Jesus. He said *no* to the hill, where they had crucified him. He said *no* to the grave where they had buried him. And that *no* meant that you didn't have to settle down in the grim facts—the Cross was the worst of them!—or in any of these spotty little anecdotes that seem to make up our life—not in a world where Christmas comes out of a stable, and the Son of God out of a little village, and twenty centuries of Christianity out of a tomb.

That *no* meant something they wanted it to mean about them, too. You remember how we all looked to Philip Wylie, in his *Generation of Vipers*—claws and jaws and stomachs, not much else—and how he undertook then to write a book about the kind of moral life we had to build with that for a foundation. With all the evidence he had, and more in the face of it, Jesus laid everybody out on such a different blueprint. Have you ever seen those massive figures there in Florence, still bound in the crude stone from which Michelangelo's chisel has only here and there released them? You would think they were writhing to be rid of the unshaped marble, trying to throw it off with their hands, struggling to get their feet out of it. Jesus saw Mary of Magdala that way, and Peter on the shores of Galilee, and Zacchaeus down in Jericho. He knew that none of us could ever safely be treated as less than we are, our hunger and our thirst, our eternal destiny, drawn out in every straining muscle! If the cross had been the end of it, I suppose the disciples would still have remembered how he had flung his gallant promises around in the very teeth of the gale that whipped away his breath—calling out hopes that had long since been dead, getting them up from their forgotten graves—but if death had stopped his mouth, they would have known who the winner was, for all his fine language. Now he stood there looking at them, as one might look out on the sea. Do you know what it did for them? They were such little folk, but his eyes were so sure they had it in them, that their fear didn't matter any more, or their running away, or the poor showing they had made. Read the story of the martyrs—that's what it did for them. By this undefeated Life—what else could it mean?—they were as great that night as ever they could bear to be—greater than they would have liked if they had known.

## II

But that brings me, you see, to the other half of this strange Gospel, the half that runs the other way. There's something about it we don't like, that keeps us from playing it down to the level of fish and chips and immortality. Maybe that's why there's so much dramatic excitement in John: people are fighting off a kind of life. They don't mind the length of it. Everlasting is all right. It's the quality which John calls eternal—that's what they can't stand! They crucified Jesus not because they liked what he said, but because they couldn't "take it" ! In one of Eugene O'Neill's plays, the Lazarus whom Jesus had raised from the dead laughs softly at the townsfolk there in Bethany, as out of a vision, like a man in love with God, saying, "There is no death!" And his laughter makes their ears drunk. The light in his eyes is a flame, and like moths they dart toward it, only to reel and turn—for they dare not come too near! Until at last like madmen they rush upon him and put him away, and hide him in the grave again. How else can men forget the God in them, lest remembrance imply too high a duty?

It takes a touch of gallantry to live in a world where things are no longer as they seem, where every one of our perspectives, as in some modernist painting, has been tossed about by this incredible thing; and the big, with which we are thoroughly at home,

199

turns out to be uncomfortably little; and what we are sure is little, nothing more than a cup of cold water, seems all at once so intolerably big. And you are told how lightly you have to sit now by the poor things you're giving your life to. Your goods are gone over, and everything you try to seem to others, while you yourself live far away inside with everything you know you are. Lazarus turned upside down everybody's idea of what was what and who was who in Palestine; and all the men and women who loved their solemn affairs thrust their fingers in their ears. Why can't we be left alone in this world that makes such good, hard sense, whose ways we understand, to hold fast our bargains? Maybe that's what we're doing anyway, holding fast to our pitiful bargains, because this isn't the gospel we really want.

Do we want it to go on pitching all our notions higher even than any of us has ever dared to pitch them? Anatole France thought there was one thing of which we could be absolutely sure, that men are always smaller than they seem. The trouble with the Easter story is that it makes them bigger than they care to be! Some people say we betake ourselves to this faith of ours because it's a kind of antidote for our cosmic insignificance. It gives us some fictitious stature under the stars! But is it stature we're after? Watch the man who comes to New York from the town back home, where he taught the men's Bible class, and all the customers in the barbershop marked his down-sitting and his uprising; watch him scuttle for cover as if he'd found him a rabbit warren where he could hide out from all the things he doesn't wish to be involved in any longer. Nobody knows him here, thank God; and nobody pays much attention to anything he's doing, thank God again! If we should start living as big as we are, we'd have to be brave enough to live even in New York as sons of God, even on Broadway at night; and when we aren't loved, to go on loving without fear! Is that what we want?

### III

"Then . . . came Jesus and stood in the midst." Half of it I like, and half of it I don't; and I have to turn it over now and then just to keep from feeling that I've been fed a two-pound box of sweet chocolates! The Columbia student that I mentioned said he had heard a few sermons that left him whispering to himself as he went out of church, "That's true, but I wish it weren't!" The fact, is, however, that both the half I like and the half I don't come to their point in this: that in any case I have to go on doing something about it. It's the surest way I have of knowing that I'm aware not just of life but of God. Things keep reminding me of him.

In the entrance to the Jan Hus church, over in the East Seventies, there is a photograph of what is said to be a dark hillside covered with patches of snow. And that's what it looks like—chance, meaningless, scattered blobs of white on black. But as you keep staring at it, quite mystified—because the caption tells you there's more in it than this—you see in three-quarters' profile a face, with high lights and shadows; and you wonder why you'd never seen it before. You can't ever again miss seeing it! It's the face of One who always has left men uneasy. Catch sight of it in the world, and you have to begin doing something about it, if no more than trying to lose sight of it again. And losing sight of it isn't easy!

Pär Lagerkvist, the Swedish poet and thinker who won the Nobel Prize for Literature in 1951, has set down in a little novel called *Barabbas* how hard it is. The story is about how the robber they swapped for Jesus was haunted by that face—a face so strong that only in weakness could it have its own way. It haunted him there in the copper mines, where he was sent soon afterward. It haunted him in the years that followed, over in Nero's Rome where at last, as he thought, he made up his mind. He would help the Savior of these Christians to set the whole of that odious world on fire—and so was farthest away when he was sure he was nearest. They arrested him and crucified him with the others, but over there to one side, because they knew he didn't really belong. And when he felt death approaching, "that which he had always been so afraid of, he said out into the darkness," as though he were speaking to it; addressing the night itself: "To thee I deliver up my soul." And you wonder. Maybe he had remembered this from Calvary, and it wasn't to the night he was speaking at all, or to the dark! And you know you're not going to find it easy to get away either. Or do you want to? Maybe that's the first bit of real evidence you'll ever have that you too have met him. Just the knowledge that there has to be more now!

But what? Not just the peace that Jesus uttered. It was too queer a brand to come just by uttering it. That night, outside, the turmoil went on. Nothing got better anywhere. Things got worse. Nothing anywhere in the years was secure. Nothing certain. Do you call that peace? Ecclesiastes had swung off down every road looking for it; and he has left us the record of his search. He looked for it in pleasure, and could have found it in his heart to hate life. He looked for it in labor, and could have found it in his heart to envy the dead. "Peace be unto thee."

The ugly sound of the present still in their ears and the grim future they saw every time they took their hands away from their eyes—what sense did it make? Peace couldn't come that way! Not while they thought there was anything left in the world worth doing. You might as well say, "Oh, come now, cheer up," to a child on a long, rainy day, with his nose pressed against the windowpane. Peace had to come this way, if you wanted it really, you decide. "As my Father hath sent me"—God had hurled him like a spear in the world's face, that's what the word means; and it hadn't been at all safe! There had been a cross there at the end. You had to make up your mind, for it or against it. "Even so [those terrible words!] send I you." (John 20:21.)

But maybe we aren't ready for that yet. Peter wasn't. What peace came to him had to come later on, up by the lake, out of the agony of his repentance, and the bitter, bitter mercy of God: "Lovest thou me?" Three times, once for every denial. It's enough to break your heart! And when you ask him, because he knows and you don't, "Lord, do I love thee?" he doesn't answer, says Kierkegaard, but only keeps wanting to know how the case stands with you, saying over and over, "Feed my sheep," as if you couldn't tell any other way! Warning you too perhaps, as he warned Peter, in the lovingkindness that was his judgment, of how life meanwhile and death still have you surrounded. Said he that day, "When thou shalt be old, thou shall stretch forth thy hands, and another shall gird thee, and carry thee whither thou wouldest not." (John 21:18.) Peace would come that way. You had to decide! And when Peter wanted to know how it would be with John, all he got was, "What is that to thee? follow thou me."

Date any of it where you think it ought to be dated. With this Love in here that has broken through—maybe it's the only thing that ever can!—and that wide gesture toward the life out yonder! "As my Father hath sent me." Whatever the future holds, it won't be dull on those terms. So he "breathed on them," that night in Jerusalem, and said, "Receive ye the Holy Ghost" (John 20:22). Can you date that? There's no magic about it. It's just the assurance that God doesn't need to have you on his hands anymore; you can have him on yours, if you prefer it that way, with more than the memory of a face and the echo of strange words that flout us with what isn't true, and we wish it were—or with what is true, and we wish it weren't. You say which it is to be! In the ancient art of India, the Buddha never appears: only the footprints which mark his passing. That doesn't have to be the tragedy of any life.

Andrew over yonder in the corner; James and John by the table; Matthew, Bartholomew, Philip, and Thomas now! Figure out their chances sometime; then range them by the side of yours!

# CONTRIBUTORS

HAMPTON ADAMS is minister of the Park Avenue Christian Church (Disciples of Christ), New York, New York.

JOHN SUTHERLAND BONNELL is minister of the Fifth Avenue Presbyterian Church, New York, New York, and in charge of National Vespers and Pilgrimage, network programs of the American Broadcasting Company.

HAROLD A. BOSLEY is minister of the First Methodist Church, Evanston, Illinois.

JOHN R. BROKHOFF is minister of St. Mark's Lutheran Church, Charlotte, North Carolina.

JOHN L. CASTEEL is Professor of Practical Theology at Union Theological Seminary, New York, New York. He is an ordained minister of the Congregational Christian Church.

ALBERT EDWARD DAY is minister of the Mount Vernon Place Methodist Church, Baltimore, Maryland.

THEODORE PARKER FERRIS is rector of Trinity Church, Boston, Massachusetts.

ROBERT E. GOODRICH, JR., is minister of the First Methodist Church, Dallas, Texas.

RALPH A. HERRING is minister of the First Baptist Church, Winston-Salem, North Carolina.

GERALD KENNEDY is resident bishop of the Los Angeles Area of The Methodist Church.

DAVID A. MacLENNAN is minister of the Brick Presbyterian Church, Rochester, New York.

DONALD MACLEOD is Professor of Homiletics and Worship at Princeton Theological Seminary, Princeton, New Jersey.

DUKE K. McCALL is President of the Southern Baptist Theological Seminary, Louisville, Kentucky.

CLIFFORD ANSGAR NELSON is minister of the Gloria Dei Lutheran Church, St. Paul, Minnesota, and chaplain of the state senate.

WILLIAM EVERETTE PHIFER, JR., is minister of the First Presbyterian Church, Monrovia, California.

HAROLD COOKE PHILLIPS is minister of the First Baptist Church, Cleveland, Ohio.

DAVID H. C. READ is minister of the Madison Avenue Presbyterian Church, New York, New York.

JOHN A. REDHEAD is minister of the First Presbyterian Church, Greensboro, North Carolina.

PAUL S. REES is minister of the First Covenant Church, Minneapolis, Minnesota.

PAUL SCHERER is Professor of Homiletics at Union Theological Seminary, New York, New York.

ROLLAND W. SCHLOERB is minister of the Hyde Park Baptist Church, Chicago, Illinois.

SAMUEL M. SHOEMAKER is rector of the Calvary Episcopal Church, Pittsburgh, Pennsylvania.

JOSEPH R. SIZOO is Professor of Religion and Director of the Chapel at George Washington University, Washington, D. C.

RALPH W. SOCKMAN is minister of Christ Church (Methodist), New York City, and is preacher of the National Radio Pulpit of the National Broadcasting Company.